Twayne's United States Authors Series

Sylvia E. Bowman, *Editor*

INDIANA UNIVERSITY

Floyd   Dell

FLOYD DELL

By JOHN E. HART

Albion College

(TUSAS) 184

Twayne Publishers, Inc. :: New York.

TO MARY HELEN

Acknowledgments

Acknowledgment is made to Amy Nyholm, Manuscript Librarian at the Newberry Library, for permission to quote from "The Floyd Dell collection in the Newberry Library, Chicago, Illinois," and with permission of Floyd Dell; to G. Thomas Tanselle for permission to quote from his dissertation, "Faun at the Barricades" (Northwestern University, 1959); and to *The Western Humanities Review* for the use of material from my essay on Floyd Dell in the Winter issue, 1962.

Acknowledgment is also made to the following publishers and writers for permission to use quotations from the works named:

Appleton-Century of Meredith Press: from *Chicago Renaissance* by Dale Kramer, copyright 1966 by Dale Kramer.

Doubleday and Company: from *Were You Ever a Child?, Moon-Calf, The Briary-Bush, Janet March, This Mad Ideal, Looking at Life, Runaway, Intellectual Vagabondage, Love in Greenwich Village, An Old Man's Folly, An Unmarried Father, Souvenir* by Floyd Dell. Copyright 1919; 1920 and (c) 1957 by Floyd Dell; 1921 and (c) 1957 by Floyd Dell; 1923 and Revised edition, 1927; 1924, 1925; 1925; 1926; 1926; 1926; 1927; 1929.

Harcourt, Brace & World, Inc.: from *Writers on the Left* by Daniel Aaron, copyright 1961 by Daniel Aaron; *Midwest Portraits* by Harry Hansen, copyright 1923; *Bygones* by Louis Untermeyer, copyright 1965 by Louis Untermeyer.

Harper and Row: from *Enjoyment of Living* by Max Eastman, copyright 1948 by Max Eastman.

Holt, Rinehart and Winston, Inc.: from *Diana Stair, The Golden Spike, Homecoming, Love in the Machine Age,* and *Love Without Money* by Floyd Dell. Copyright 1930, 1931, 1932, 1933, 1934, (c) 1958, 1959, 1960, 1961, 1962 by Floyd Dell. Reprinted by permission of Holt, Rinehart and Winston, Inc. From *An American Testament* by Joseph Freeman, copy-

Houghton Mifflin Company: from *Romantic Rebels* by Emily Hahn, copyright 1966 by Emily Hahn.

Random House, Inc.: from *Love and Revolution* by Max Eastman, copyright 1964 by Max Eastman.

Floyd Dell's generosity in supplying information and in reading and commenting on the manuscript has been especially appreciated. I am particularly grateful to William J. Henneman, Bookseller, Chicago, for his cheerful help in obtaining hard-to-find copies of Dell's writings; to Mrs. Amy Nyholm at the Newberry Library for her gracious assistance in making the Dell manuscripts available; to Albion College for a one semester sabbatical leave to work on the project; to Elizabeth Hosmer, Albion College, and Lotus Snow, Keuka College, for reading the manuscript; and to Sylvia Bowman for the careful editing that the manuscript so justly needed; and to my wife, whose help made the project possible.

Preface

When Floyd Dell retired from government service in 1947, he had been an active part of the American intellectual and literary scene for nearly fifty years; yet his writings have fallen into relative obscurity since the early 1930's. His long and distinguished career has included that of reporter, literary and social critic, editor, dramatist, essayist, poet, novelist and, as he has said, "minor bureaucrat." In the 1920's he had already become something of a legend to newer Greenwich Villagers who thought of him as the archetypal Bohemian of pre-World War I days. Born in the heartland of America, self-educated in the social and literary movements of his time, Dell had made his own way: he had helped to create and sustain what was later called the "Chicago literary renaissance." He later became one of the leading spokesmen in New York's Greenwich Village, an editor, dramatist, and critic; during the 1920's and 1930's, beginning with *Moon-Calf,* he published eleven novels and became one of the important novelists of the era. In the mid-1930's, prompted by economic necessity, he took a position as writer and editor in a government agency. In a sense, these four major episodes in his life were a continuing part of what he called an "intellectual pilgrimage." That pilgrimage had taken him from a small village in Illinois to Davenport, Iowa; Chicago; New York; and, finally, Washington.

If Dell had never become a novelist, his place in the history of modern literature would have been secure. As associate editor and then editor of the Chicago *Evening Post Friday Literary Review,* he had championed social causes and the new literary Realism and had played a vital part in Chicago's cultural revival. As managing editor of the newly organized *Masses* magazine and later of *The Liberator,* Dell had become well known in New York not only for his liberal ways, but for his radical social thinking, his political acumen, his contribution to the Liberal

Club and Provincetown Players, his expert knowledge of books and writers. Editor, critic, playwright, he had become, some said, the foremost book reviewer in America. And while he continued his editorial chores well into the 1920's and never ceased to write essays, reviews, and poetry even into the 1960's, he reestablished himself in a sense through a new career as novelist in 1920.

During the 1920's and before, Dell's writing had already received considerable notice from contemporaries; and in recent years his part as a radical thinker, especially during the Chicago and Greenwich Village days, has received considered and judicious treatment by Daniel Aaron, Bernard Duffey, Allen Churchill, Emily Hahn, and Dale Kramer. But Dell the writer, especially Dell the novelist has been barely mentioned. With the exception of several unpublished doctoral dissertations on Dell's life and writings, no full-length study has yet appeared. This study is, I think, long overdue.

My aim has been to examine both Dell's life and his writings and to give major attention to his novels. Actually, Dell's own life is inextricably linked with his thought and ideas; whether in essay, critical review, or novel, he drew heavily on his own experience in everything he wrote. Nearly all of his writing, but especially his novels, clearly emerged from his early life and from events of the Chicago and first years in Greenwich Village. To understand his point of view is to know something of his life in small towns in mid-America and to know a life of economic privation, thwarted hopes, and vague dreams. Long before Dell's family moved to Davenport, Iowa, his "intellectual pilgrimage" was underway. In Davenport, he made friends with writers and thinkers; he met Socialists and anarchists. With amazing self-direction and discipline, he read widely and began to write for newspapers and magazines. In Chicago, his first marriage began and ended; his radical thinking had, in part, brought personal frustration, but his success as critic and editor had given him a national reputation. Dell's sojourn in Greenwich Village, his indictment for conspiracy against the government with other editors of *The Masses* and the subsequent trials, his Bohemian ways, and his common-sense thinking—all these aspects of his life became the basis for a personal point of view that he maintained throughout his writing, and particularly in his novels. Working in the tradition of Daniel Defoe and Charles Reade, of Mark Twain, Count Tolstoi, and Arnold Bennett, he shaped personal experience and events into a fictional representation of real life.

While this study is chiefly organized chronologically, I have sometimes departed from a strict time sequence when continuity of discussion seemed to justify it. Dell did not, for example, write the story of Felix Fay as a trilogy. The third episode in Felix's life followed some nine years after his appearance in *Moon-Calf* in 1920, but I have considered the whole story in Chapter 4. And in Chapter 6, which pieces together the tangle of Dell's work on *The Liberator* and examines his plays, essays, and critical writings, there is an over-lapping of dates, for the volumes appeared at intervals throughout the 1920's and sometimes in the same year as the novels. Within the chapter, I have followed a time sequence. I have also used quotations, especially from Dell's own writings, rather generously, since his work is today generally unknown and is sometimes unavailable.

Although the novels receive considerable attention, I have nonetheless aimed to show the extent of Dell's contribution to American letters. My purpose has been to avoid as much as possible duplication of thought and idea in the many reviews and essays and to present a less detailed picture of his writing during the Chicago and Greenwich Village days. Yet, except for several pamphlets on marriage and education, the published volumes are duly noted. What is neglected in this study are his poetry, most of it still in manuscript in the Newberry Library, and many essays, some of them still unpublished or published in magazines not readily available.

In analyzing Dell's life and writings, I have aimed to examine the nature of his "intellectual pilgrimage," the progress of an intellectual and idealist, whose joys and griefs in life and love led to the realization that man must of necessity learn to adapt himself to the ordinary world of which he is a part. No other writer of the 1920's has expressed with such wistful poignancy the maturation of the young and sensitive intellectual who finds himself sometimes isolated and alone in the towns and cities of mid-America. A central problem of that process was, Dell thought, finding love and marriage in the changing world of the machine. What he personally thought and felt to be true, he "dramatized" in the novels and declared in personal essays and criticism. But his writing is more than reflection of personal problems and sensitivity to changing mores; it reflects the frustrations and anxieties of the many who live in a society where those problems still remain—and are still unsolved.

Contents

Chronology

1887   Floyd James Dell born June 18, Barry, Illinois.

1889   Dell family moves to Quincy, Illinois, in late summer.

1903   Joins Socialist party in summer; moves with family to Davenport, Iowa.

1904   Does not return to high school in the fall. Meets Fred Feuchter. Works in Socialist party.

1905   Cub reporter on Davenport *Times.*

1906   Edits several issues of *Tri-City Workers'* Magazine. Reporter on Davenport *Democrat.* With George Cook, founds the Monist Society.

1908   In autumn, goes to Chicago to look for a job; reporter on Chicago *Evening Post.*

1909   Assistant to Francis Hackett, editor, of the new *Friday Literary Review* supplement of Chicago *Evening Post.* In August, marries Margery Currey, Evanston, Illinois.

1910   In January, associate editor of *Friday Literary Review.*

1911   In July, editor of *Friday Literary Review.*

1913   Dells move to Fifty-seventh Street district in April. By end of summer he and his wife separate. Dell leaves Chicago for New York in autumn. Publishes first book, *Women as World Builders.*

1914   Becomes associate editor of *The Masses* in January. Contributes one-act plays to Liberal Club.

1916   Contributes plays to the Provincetown Players in the Village.

1917   Suppression of *The Masses.* Begins visits to psychoanalyst in autumn. In November *The Masses* ends publication.

1918   Max and Crystal Eastman founded *The Liberator* in March; Dell associate editor. First *Masses* Trial in April. Drafted into the army on June 27; discharged ten days later. Second *Masses* Trial in October. Publishes *The Angel Intrudes* (play).

1919   Marries Berta-Marie Gage in February. Publishes *Were You Ever a Child?* in September.

1920   *Moon-Calf* in September.

1921   *The Briary-Bush* in November; *Sweet and Twenty* (play).

1922   First son, Anthony, born in January. Publishes *King Arthur's Socks and Other Village Plays.*

1923   *Janet March* in August.

1924   *Looking at Life* in April. *The Liberator* suspends publication in October. *Janet March* suppressed.

1925   *This Mad Ideal* in February. Travels in England and France during summer. *Runaway* in September.

1926   *Intellectual Vagabondage* in March; *Love in Greenwich Village* in May; *An Old Man's Folly* in October.

1927   *Upton Sinclair* in July; *An Unmarried Father* in September; Burton's *The Anatomy of Melancholy* (with Paul Jordan-Smith) in December. Revision of *Janet March.* Second son, Christopher, born in September.

1928   Lecture tour, Pacific coast. *Little Accident* (with Thomas Mitchell) opens October 9 at Morosco Theatre in New York for extended run.

1929   *Souvenir* in February.

1930   *Love in the Machine Age* in April. *Little Accident* made into a movie.

1931   Buys summer place in New Hampshire in February. Speaks at International Mental Hygiene Congress in Washington in May. Lecture tour during June in Chicago and Cleveland. *Cloudy with Showers* (with Thomas Mitchell) opens September 1 for seventy-one performances. *Love Without Money* in October.

1932   *Diana Stair* in October. Lecture tour.

1933   *Homecoming* in September.

1934   *The Golden Spike* in October.

1935   Accepts appointment in Washington with Works Progress Administration doing editorial work.

1941-   Travels widely for WPA, observing and making notes
1942   on various projects.

1947   Retires from government work. Does free-lance writing.

1950   Readies over 3600 items for Floyd Dell Collection in Newberry Library, Chicago.

1953   Reads tribute to William Butler Yeats over radio station WCFM, Washington, D. C., in March.

1969   Celebrates fiftieth wedding anniversary in February. Dies July 23, Bethesda, Maryland.

CHAPTER 1

The Early Years

REBELLION has always played a key role in man's intellectual, moral, and esthetic progress. It has formulated much of his social, political, and artistic thinking; it has inspired young intellectuals and artists to wander forth into new realms of desires and imaginative concepts. In one way or another, Floyd Dell's thought and writings are impelled by a rebellious spirit that manifests itself in political, social, and literary radicalism. Yet, for one who was both a political revolutionary and a rebellious Bohemian, his writings, and especially his novels, seem today, because of our social changes, rather old-fashioned and unduly sensible. Rebellion for him was a way of returning to fundamental aspects of life in a rapidly changing world.

I *In Barry*

Floyd Dell was born June 28, 1887, in Barry, Illinois, a small town not far from the Mississippi River. His father, of Pennsylvania Dutch, and his mother, of Irish Protestant stock, were both in their forties when Dell was born. Dell's father, an Illinois cavalryman, had been wounded and captured in Texas during the Civil War. After his release from a Southern prison camp, he returned to Barry and went into the butcher business. He married; the business prospered; and the Dell family, two sons and a daughter, seemed securely members of that class which "was, in Pike County, and perhaps all through America, called 're-spectable.' "[1] But life in the changing world of growing America was not always easy.

Long before Dell was born, the family had had financial reverses. The butcher shop had ceased to exist; Dell's father, often out of work, had had to settle for odd jobs. The two older brothers, who dropped out of school because "they didn't like to wear patched clothes," found what work they could and helped: one brother, a sensitive artist, became a harnessmaker; the other, good at figures, worked in a sash-and-door factory. The family managed; and, while it clung all the more to its respectable status, it was "losing its hold upon the golden ladder."[2] Although Dell later recalled that he had had the finest father a boy could have—one who had taught his son the manual of arms, encouraged political aspirations in the Republican party, told stories that he would recall having heard many times over—the young Dell was sometimes "cruelly disillusioned" with a father who seemed "no model, no hero," and whose authority he sometimes defied.

"Shy, energetic, and a lover of poetry," Dell's mother belonged to what her son called his "Ideal Universe." Once a schoolteacher, she recognized the boy's quickness in memory, his grasp of ideas, and his vocabulary as hopefully signifying the sharp intelligence of a future scholar. Like many American mothers, she was the moral authority of the family, "the Lawgiver," "an all-powerful Goddess." It was she who provided the moral universe, that "Picture of the World," for which the boy dreamed: a world of manners and order, a world of what had become for the Dells only "pretenses of prosperous respectability." This ideal world was not always directly related to the one of fact.

By the time Dell was six years old, he was, he remembers, "an arrogant, eager, friendly, confident, innocently bumptious little boy." He learned easily, had a "prodigious memory," could read before he was five. On his first day of school he corrected the teacher who was giving them military drill: he "told her she must say 'Fire!' and not 'Shoot!'" Yet, out of "loyalty and obedience" to his mother and to his teacher, he wanted to do right, to be good. On the playground, he learned that some children were not nice to play with, and he discovered that "in the currency of 'respectability' a father who used to have a butcher shop was not quite on a par with a father who was cashier of the bank."[3]

He remembered always the impoverished Christmas of 1893: his father had been out of work; they had eaten potato soup every day. The oldest son was in Quincy; the others were with relatives. No one had mentioned Christmas, until on Christmas

Eve he had asked the day. Going to bed in the dark, he felt the pain in his body ebb as the one in his mind began: "I *knew*. . . . I knew why I hadn't gone to school that fall—why I hadn't any new shoes—why we had been living on potato soup all winter. . . . *'We're poor!'* " That poverty had been concealed from him. He saw now with the "cold recognition of a situation." Adjustments had to be made, and he adjusted to the new awareness by renouncing, as he recalls, "many familiar expectations": "I had wanted (something) for Christmas. I didn't want it, now. I didn't want anything." As wishes shriveled and died with the "cold emotion of renunciation," the boy confronted the nothingness before him: "I would never let myself want anything again."[4] The event left an effect on his attitude toward life.

In a sense, the renunciation had changed the boy's point of view. Although he wandered around the village square, watched boys play marbles, listened to idlers telling stories, and even played with those of his own age in the real world of "lawless fact," he was much more at home in the world of books and art —a world that was really an extension of that "Ideal Universe" which his mother had helped to shape for him.[5] As he writes, ". . . before I came to anything as I went further and further into the world, before I could hear it, see it, smell it, touch it, taste it, I had it already in my mind, in its place among other things, explained and understood in advance. Books were taking up the work; the Ideal Universe grew every day larger, brighter, more orderly, more understandable, more complete."[6]

As books helped to expand young Dell's Ideal Universe, so did he find a refuge of order in a diversity of reading. He liked stories of both imaginary and real life: he fell in love with *The Arabian Nights*; he "adored" the scientific fantasies of Jules Verne. He liked poems "that could be recited aloud, like 'Sheridan's Ride' and 'Barbara Frietchie.' . . ." Mark Twain's *A Connecticut Yankee* left "a permanent democratic contempt for medieval glories"; *Innocents Abroad,* a "scorn for all that was still medieval-aristocratic in modern Europe"; and *The Prince and the Pauper,* he said, "made it easier for me to become a Socialist in my adolescence." From Defoe and Charles Reade Dell learned "something about the world I lived in," as he did not from the "unreal books of Dickens and Thackeray."[7] By the time he was twelve, he had discovered ancient Greece, which he liked "so much better than the factory town to which my family had moved, that I lived in the past rather than in the present."[8]

Yet the present intruded: a growing awareness of sex, the facts of life found in a "doctor book," the realities of daydreams were also shaping the inner life of the sensitive boy. He learned about egotism: he had written his name in big chalk letters on the house where he was born. When the principal of the school found out what he had done, he presented the boy's action to the class as an example of egotism. Dell was embarrassed, dismayed, and defiant. When his brother went into the Spanish-American War, he fancied himself a "war-correspondent . . . one who took photographs." He read about two girls in the Frank Merriwell dime-novel series, one who seemed good, but was not, and one who was thought bad, but was good. It was a "problem of profound importance" to him: how did one know the good from the bad? And, as realities of the present fused with realities in books, Dell turned to his world of dreams and fantasies. Then, in 1899, the family left Barry and moved to the larger town of Quincy.

II *In Quincy*

In a sense, moving to Quincy meant a partial severance from the past and a hopeful beginning, a pattern of development and renewal that characterized both Dell's own life and the lives of many characters in his novels. The past, of course, was never completely shut out: as he remembers, the thirty years' collection of household pieces made the house in Quincy "look like all the houses we had ever lived in."

But life in Quincy was also one of personal discovery and growth. Young Dell had brought his appetite for reading, his curiosity for the exotic, the moral, the scientific. He dreamed of becoming an explorer; he read travel folders and wandered about Quincy. At Franklin School, he organized the Literary and Athletic Society; and in June, 1900, he delivered an oration at the graduation exercises. He began to collect a personal library that included Emerson's *Essays,* Carlyle's *Past and Present,* Ik

[Donald Grant Mitchell] Marvel's *Reveries of a Bachelor.* He joined the Presbyterian Church; but, after reading Robert G. Ingersoll, he became an atheist. Indignant when a lady bookseller wheedled money from his mother for some books, he tried to replace the amount by selling books himself.

From a number of writers he began to learn about socialism. He read Edward Bellamy's *Looking Backward,* William Morris's *News from Nowhere,* George Kennan's "tremendous magazine articles on Russia, the Nihilists, and Siberia." From Ignatius Donnelly's popular pseudo-scientific book on Plato's lost Atlantis and from his sensational Populist novel *Caesar's Column,* full of violence and horrors about the world's future if changes in the socio-economic situation were not made, Dell gained, he thought, "a more realistic notion of revolution than . . . from current Socialist Party propaganda. . . ."[9] When he heard a "street sweeper" talking socialism, he joined the Socialist local and read the "Communist Manifesto." He was barely sixteen.

Atheist, nihilist, Socialist—member of the working class—Dell was a long way from the pattern of life and ideas of sober respectability. "Revolutionary literature" seemed a salvation: it provided "an imaginative world," he recalls, "in which considerations of respectability and manners did not count, and in which heroism was conceived as being directed to the creation of a better world. . . ." Such devotion to a "cause" relieved him of a "burden of obligation" to his mother and to his own conscience; it released him from the idea that his father was "morally culpable" in having failed to keep the family in respectable comfort.[10] A devotion to "cause" helped salve "an old wound" —as Dell calls his grudge—but the facts of his past remained. He was sensitive about poverty for many years, even after a Bohemian life had returned him to the pattern of middle-class respectability and morality.

During summers in Quincy, he had a variety of jobs: he was a bundle boy for a department store, an elevator boy, a helper in a harness factory, a book-canvasser. In the summer of 1903 he worked in a candy factory. He fell in love with one of the girls there and even thought of her in terms of marriage. Then, at end of summer, the family moved to Davenport, Iowa, where Dell gained both a direction and a profession. If life in

Quincy nurtured a world in which problems of respectability,
rebellion, and hope for the future might be resolved in theory,
life in Davenport offered ways to solve them in fact. Here the
boy's talent for writing became the tool of a profession that
would enable him to rebel, yet help create a new and different
world from the one he had known, and to achieve, partly on his
own terms, a bright future that brought him both recognition
and success.

III *In Davenport*

In 1903 Davenport was a growing city of tree-shaded streets
and fine buildings, with all the dignity and bravado of an old
river port. Its two sister cities across the river—Rock Island and
Moline—were a nightmare of industrialism and rail tracks, of
workmen's houses, and of the contrasting castles of great barons
of finance. Davenport, with its German and Jewish population
and its touches of Old World charm, was liberal, cosmopolitan.
There were several daily newspapers; and, as Dell was to discover, an intelligentsia that included such known and to-be-
known writers as Octave Thanet, Arthur Davison Ficke, George
Cram Cook, Harry Hansen, and Susan Glaspell. Dell was to form
lifelong friendships with most of these writers.

Although Dell dropped out of high school in Davenport without graduating, learning became for him a continuing process of
self-education. For example, he read and memorized English
poetry—Wordsworth, Shelley, Tennyson, Housman—"at the rate
of one great poet a week." He attended Socialist meetings in
Turner Hall. He went often to the public library, where he met
librarian Marilla Freeman, a devotee of Emerson; she became
his friend and urged the young poet to consider writing as a profession. He met Charles Banks, a local poet and journalist, who
"taught me," Dell recalls, "patiently how to criticize my own
work, and how to revise it. . . ."[11] He lost a chance to attend
college when he "blasted college education with a withering fire
of criticism" to the very person who would have been his bene-
factor. Dell thought then—and later—that "the actualities of life
were the only school in which one could learn to write."[12]

Harry Hansen remembers Dell as a "lean lad," "rather negli-

gent of his clothes and somewhat diffident in his manner. . . ."
Although "unobtrusive in a group," he could talk fluently if
someone "hit his subject": "Strange comment on philosophy;
quotations from poets with unfamiliar names; stories from
books with unconventional foreign titles."[13] He read about science and socialism; observantly, he prowled the streets of Davenport; he worked in a candy factory; he wrote poetry; and all of
his experiences contributed to his education and development.
His first printed poem, "Memorial Day," appeared in the local
newspaper in the spring of 1904.

Already a Socialist, Dell met at one of the local meetings,
Fred Feuchter, a mail-carrier well versed in Socialist doctrine.
His friendship with Feuchter was, he said later, "the most important thing that had happened in my life." Feuchter taught
him not to "pre-judge life, but to take it as it came and see it as
it was."[14] "What I learned. . . ," Dell recalls, "were practical,
sensible ways of dealing with the world—attitudes, rather than
specific things, and really but simple common-sense."[15] Here
were heady lessons for a young idealist with poetic inclinations.
As Socialist, Dell wrestled with the "conflict between parlia-
mentarianism and direct economic action as preached by the
I.W.W." He read G. K. Chesterton, "whose reactionary religious and other social tendencies puzzled" him, but served as cor-
rective to his enthusiasm for George Bernard Shaw.[16] Under the
aegis of socialism, Dell's "world of forward-looking ideas" began to unify as intellectualized concepts, ones not always related to the human condition. After Feuchter had urged him to
use his mind to make a living, Dell went to the Davenport
Times, asked for a job, and was hired immediately. He did not
know that an advertisement for a cub reporter had just appeared
in the last edition of the paper.

Dell began his newspaper career in January, 1905, on the
Davenport *Times,* but he was fired within a month because he
had no "nose for news." Given two weeks' notice, he worked
hard and dug up several "human interest stories" a day; as a result, he was reinstated. Later, mostly under pseudonyms, he
published a few "muckraking" stories in a local Socialist paper,
the *Tri-City Workers' Magazine;* and what concerned him then—
conditions in the candy factory, the public library, the schools

in Davenport, socialism and the working classes—he later used in essays and fiction.

In August, 1906, he became for several issues the editor of the magazine and made the masthead read: "A Fearless Journal of Current Events and Economic Principles." Editorials emphasized the need for courage among Socialist members, attacked the "noisome garbage dump" in Moline, or implicated respectable citizens in Nick Bingo's dancehall and the red-light district that is "built on the profit system." The *Times,* which had hardly approved of his articles, fired him; but almost immediately Ralph Cram, editor of the Davenport *Democrat,* offered him a job.

Actually, Dell found straight reporting a highly impersonal business. He preferred the kind of writing and news gathering that enabled him to use his "own opinions, feelings, convictions and tastes."[17] Thus, his "Socialist" journalism became both "escape from" and "protest against"—a kind of spiritual relief from reporting that was "sans taste, sans guts, sans principles, sans feelings, sans damn near everything that made life worth living."[18] Partly through interviews connected with reporting, Dell continued to meet people. When he and Rabbi Fineshriber became fast friends, the rabbi encouraged young Dell's flair for dramatic criticism. At the Fineshriber home, where the two engaged in endless discussions, they were sometimes joined by Marilla Freeman, Susan Glaspell, George Cook, and Arthur Ficke. For the young poet and Socialist with a flair for ideas, the conversation and company were vastly stimulating.

Dell was also writing articles and criticism, drama and poetry, and love letters. His play, *Sinners All,* which he destroyed, was regarded by Cook as the "best thing of that kind since Congreve and Wycherly [*sic*]." After writing one novel and parts of another, he concluded that he was not ready to deal with long sustained fiction. *Mother Earth,* an anarchist magazine, accepted articles; *The Trident,* a local magazine, published some short stories. He sold poems to *McClure's* and *Harper's.* Life was vibrant with words and ideas and dreams.

As Dell recalls, he had already formed certain beliefs in which his ancestry may have played a role. He had a German love of "order and philosophy and thoroughness"; he had such Irish traits as love of poetry, "mysticism and undependableness and insincerity and love of showing off."[19] He felt that "Socialist views were permanently fixed in my mind"; but, if he were an "enemy of the class" to which he could and did belong, he saw that "politics was not for me."[20] He knew then, as he knew and remembered later, that "one must be *sure* that it was an impersonal end and not a selfish personal one that was being gained."[21]

Harry Hansen recalls "that Floyd's socialist activity was largely due to a lad's hunger for new intellectual contacts, a reaching out for new friendships to replace the inadequacy of association with mere schoolboys."[22] But the hunger and the reaching out had surely been impelled by the lack of economic security in his life and by his desire for respectability. To most Americans, poetry and socialism were hardly an acceptable or a practical way of achieving success; and whatever Dell's dreams and idealism, there remained the practical business of making a living, a fact which as much as any other was to be a continuing guide to his choices and decisions. As poet, Socialist, and writer, he was sometimes lonely, partly an outsider, or at best a member of a small group. With ideas that impelled him toward nonconformity, he found the company of freethinkers and Bohemians often congenial.

Reading had already helped Dell to form his own concept of Bohemian life before he became identified with it in Davenport. That concept was not one of riotous living and idiosyncrasies in sex and dress, although he wore a black scarf to save laundry bills and later in Chicago and New York dressed in fancy togs. Nor were his ideas built on the free-and-easy artistic arrogance of the French Bohemianism of a Henri Murger. Rather, the Bohemia of which Dell approved had a revolutionary quality that included fighting and dying for a cause; it had certain "middle-class qualities": a taste for "order, chiefly, and manners, and a certain degree of dignity," and a place more seclusive than showy, a "place with some outdoors in it—trees, flowers, streams, a sky."[23]

Dell's Bohemian life did, of course, embrace more than the intellectual excitement of reading books or engaging in conversations. He had been in love; he had thought of marriage; and his affairs with women had led to thoughts about seduction and "free love," about the moral honesty of an affair; and these thoughts conflicted with a "clear conscience" and self-respect. If seduction were fraught with shame, wasn't there something amiss? And in any liaison—or marriage—the coming of children surely demanded the need for responsible action from the participants. If he had "seemed to know everything out of books and be an amazing explainer," he also realized that there was a "living wisdom" which lay "more real and deep" for him to comprehend. He also knew, whatever his desires, that he could not support a wife and children: "The world that called itself real, the world of ruthless money-making and timid respectability, sweeping on so hastily toward its doom, might in accident or malice smash our happiness at any moment."[24] As with socialism, Dell's Bohemianism became part of the poetic-social idealism of a young man who, however intoxicated with the intellectual excitement around him, began to think sanely and seriously about where that excitement was leading.

Of the many significant friends Dell made in Davenport, none was more important than George Cram Cook. Cook's family was one of means and culture; Cook himself had been to Harvard University and to Heidelberg, taught at the University of Iowa, and served in the Spanish-American War; and he had concluded that "it is better a writer make his living in some other way than by writing."[25] He wanted, Dell wrote, "to live in a world which put truth and beauty first."[26] Cook lived on the family farm at Buffalo, a few miles from Davenport, where he raised vegetables and wrote. He and Dell had already met, but the acquaintance came to nothing until they met again to form a society of freethinkers in Davenport. Dell had proposed the name of Monist Society; Cook seconded the proposal; and the two were appointed to draft a manifesto. Their discussions converted Cook from his "Nietzschean-Aristocratic-anarchist philosophy" to socialism. Dell's assurance and dogmatism, his youth and self-education impressed Cook, helped to dispel the older man's gloom.

But the friendship had meaning for Dell also. In the spring of 1908, when he was fired from the newspaper "for insolence to the proprietor," and while he waited hopefully for the economy to recover from the Panic of 1907, Dell stayed with George and Mollie Cook on the farm, helping to hoe the vegetables and cultivate the plants. As Susan Glaspell remembers, "In the whole history of Iowa there has probably not been so stimulating a hired man. . . ."[27] There was talk, and there was also Cook's receptive mind. But there was also the farm with its grassy hills, its creek and shade trees, its deep woods, the peaceful sights and sounds for which the young Dell hungered. He "went on long walks at night in town, to smell the flowers, the trees, the wet earth, to see the moon riding the clouds, to feel the night. . . ."[28]

Sometimes, while Cook worked on his novel, Cook's second wife Mollie and young Dell worked in the garden. There was actually nothing questionable between them, but Cook created friction by being quarrelsome. Yet there were good conversations and good meetings in Davenport and parties at the farm, where once Dell met Margery Currey, who taught English at the Davenport High School and invited him to spend Thanksgiving with her family in Evanston since he was planning to go to Chicago. Dell and Cook remained friends for many years. They were to work together in Chicago, in New York, and in Provincetown where Cook was to leave an indelible mark on the American theater.

Early in November, 1908, out of work and unable to find a job, Dell left Davenport. Friends advised and urged him to go, and he did, with "reluctance and regret." Looking back, he remembers that he had been "eager, curious, avid of knowledge," shy, experimental, "but underneath everything else, hard." Mostly he had been concerned with himself: his relation with men had been "callous"; with women, "rather hypocritical." Actually, men and women had meant little to him compared with ideas because he "had so far taken hold of the world with my mind—the world had not itself impinged upon my emotions."[29] Armed with a letter of introduction from Marilla Freeman and with twenty dollars in his pocket, he took the train for Chicago to seek a job.

CHAPTER 2

Dell in Chicago

"I AM NOT the same boy who came up to Chicago," Dell wrote in 1913. He was, he said, "different, in being . . . let me say, more human."[1] In those five years a variety of experiences had revealed to him something about himself. He had, of course, become a successful journalist, literary critic, and editor; but he had also failed as a husband, perhaps even as a lover—and out of these successes and failures he had come to see that he could not continue the "hardness of self-confident and inexperienced youthfulness" that sometimes caused him to be cruel to friends and loved ones. He had changed; he was now less idealistic; people had become more important to him than ideas; and his growing concern for others had made him a little more like an "ordinary person." He found that coping with personal and emotional problems had pushed him from a world of art and ideas and introspection into a concern for others, a concern for ordinary life and the affairs of people.

This movement from the "ideal" to the "real," from the self to others, becomes a pattern in his life and in the lives of many characters in his novels. If the Chicago years led him to discover what "all the world has always known," he was discovering it himself and in his own way. His growing awareness and understanding of the artist's need for sympathy and compassion were to give his life and writing poignancy.

I *At the* Post

After Dell arrived in Chicago in early November, 1908, he set about finding a job. Marilla Freeman's introduction to Charles Hallinan, an editorial writer on the Chicago *Evening Post*, gave Dell a new and helpful friend who introduced him to the city editors. They allowed him to make the *Post* his headquarters and, after a while, even tried him out as a reporter. With his inventive mind, his whimsical and humorous style, which he said came in part from Margery Currey's lively and charming letters and from the graceful lightness of her conversation, he was perhaps best at writing human interest stories (as would be the hero in *Love Without Money*). The editors liked his tone of urbanity, and Hallinan, who had a social-settlement background and enlightened views, not only liked and encouraged him, but helped this shy and somewhat retiring youth emerge from his shell and become that "other vastly confident, voluble, easily friendly, somewhat arrogant and rather bumptious self."[2] For a while, Dell taught a class in English literature at Hull House. He attended the opera and concerts; saw Isadora Duncan dance; met Mrs. Elia Peattie, literary critic of the *Tribune,* and heard her read J. M. Synge; and attended a meeting in memory of the Haymarket victims. In a sense getting started, even in Chicago, had been fairly easy.

With the new century, Chicago had become a robust, expanding city. A polyglot of nationalities—a microcosm, as Bernard Duffey points out, of the nation as a whole—Chicago was diverse with races, religions, occupations, classes, conflicts. Its central location, its railroad terminals, and its cheap waterway transportation had made it the center for meat products, Pullman cars, soaps and shoes, farm implements, men's clothing, chewing gum, chemicals and canned goods, and iron and steel products. Accumulated wealth had even built museums and libraries, an opera house and orchestra hall, colleges and clubs, newspapers, and merchandizing establishments. Chicago was "a city in rushing transition—always hurrying on," the focal point of a developing region.

But there had also been changes in the mind and spirit of Chicago. The still dominant values and ideas of rural and post-Civil War America were now invaded by new voices from a world of wealth and business and growing social problems. If, as Burton Rascoe observes, Chicago in the main was "crude, vulgar, vital and grasping," there were signs of liberation. Reform and social ferment had already fanned the political air: the growth of the Socialist party, the agitations of the Populists, the reportage of the muckrakers; the social work of Jane Addams; the newspaper writings of Eugene Field, George Ade, and Finley

Peter Dunne, which protested against social degradation and poked fun at human folly. Novelists—Henry Fuller, Frank Norris, Upton Sinclair, Robert Herrick, Theodore Dreiser—continued the onslaught. As Fuller pointed out in 1897, the community needed to overcome the "dual domination of Greed and of Slouch" and to work with honesty.

The World's Fair of 1893 had presented Chicago's progress with fanfare; but there were other evidences of it: the Art Institute; the University of Chicago; the new symphony orchestra; libraries, available to all; and "The Little Room," available to some, where a group discussed literature and the arts on Friday afternoons. Francis Fisher Brown was editing the *Dial* magazine; Herbert Stone, the *Chapbook*. Already there were signs of new energy and excitement; but, when Dell came to Chicago, what has been called the "Chicago renaissance" was hardly apparent. Burton Rascoe dates its inception with the creation of the *Friday Literary Review* supplement of the Chicago *Evening Post* in March, 1909, with Francis Hackett as editor and with Floyd Dell as his assistant.[3]

II   The Friday Literary Review

Francis Hackett, the new editor of the *Friday Literary Review,* had at eighteen left his native Ireland to come to America. A Fabian Socialist and a member of the Irish Literary Revival, Hackett, having given up his study of law in New York, had come to Chicago around 1904. He had worked in Marshall Field's; lived at Hull House; then he landed a job on the *Evening Post,* where he reported, wrote editorials; and, after Henry Fuller left, he took over the position of literary editor. Hackett at twenty-five had achieved a fine unity of "artistic and intellectual interests"; his extreme liberalism had a clearly sociological bias. Early in 1909 when he was asked to plan a new literary supplement, he offered Dell, who had already reviewed for the *Post*'s literary page, a job as his assistant. Hackett had liked the young journalist's developing style, his political and literary views, his willingness to work hard. Although he warned Dell that he would have "a hell of a lot of books to review—unsigned stuff—all the dirty work,"[4] Dell accepted. He found, he has said, that he could review "from thirty to a hundred books a week, and still have time to read one book and criticize it."[5] When the initial issue of the *Review* appeared on March 5, 1909, Dell was not yet twenty-two years old.

Both conservative and forward-looking, the *Post* was heavy with financial news but somewhat advanced in taste and cultural matters. At a time when literary criticism was unusually pedantic in upholding Romantic respectability, the writings of Hackett and Dell seemed radical and rebellious. Both were social idealists; both were interested in esthetics. Their militancy rang forth like a program of change, which it partly was. A pioneer in the field, the Chicago *Evening Post Friday Literary Review* aimed to be of service both to "the book-reading public" and "to good literature": it helped formulate and encourage modern civilized criticism and literary taste in America. In bringing "social ideas to bear upon aesthetic products," the editors received an encouraging response from readers, critics, and publishers. The *Review* was fresh, original. And it sold books. Composed usually of eight tabloid-sized pages—sometimes four or sixteen— it generally reviewed an important new book on the front page. There were editorials, shorter reviews, often by specialists, and featured columns—"London Letter," "New York Letter," "Literary Small Talk," "Magazine Critique."

As editor, Hackett wrote most of the signed reviews on page one (but Dell wrote a half dozen during the first year) and probably most of the editorials. His ideas reflected his Fabian background; his style, his incisive and informed mind. His literary reviews established precedents: he saw literature as a way to the new Socialist order; he attacked raw power and smugness, greed, and waste; he suspected Jack London's brand of socialism and Mencken's estimate of Nietzsche. He admired Shaw and Ibsen, Walt Whitman, and Tolstoy; he praised H. G. Wells as a heretic, idealist, Socialist. He liked the Realism of Stephen Crane and Arnold Bennett. The editorials in the *Review*—under Hackett and later Dell—attacked complacency and stuffiness in the arts in such statements as "where are the American Galsworthy, Conrad, George Moore, Wells, Chesterton, Kipling, Arnold Bennett, J. M. Barrie, W. W. Jacobs, Eden Phillpotts?" "America has yet to conform to the ideal [Whitman] predicated"; "while the critic must judge, he must indeed understand"; or " . . . we have misgivings about the type of culture to which the *Atlantic* [*Monthly*] is devoted."

After nearly a year of apprenticeship, Dell was listed as associate editor on January 28, 1910. He had nearly two hundred items to his credit—reviews, features, editorials. Partly with Hackett's help and encouragement, he was developing a style that was warmly personal, humorous, and ironic; and he was helping to stimulate and shape the direction of literature as well as the critical attitude toward it. He says of Hackett and their contribution: "we got along very well, and did some good pioneer work on behalf of modern American literature."[6]

III *Marriage*

A second event in 1909, if clearly related to his literary career, bears more directly on Dell's personal and emotional development. In late August, he and Margery Currey were married at her home in Evanston by Rabbi Fineshriber, who came from Davenport for the occasion. Since neither was Jewish, the ceremony for them was a bit unconventional—but so was the marriage. At twenty-two, Dell was older in mind and thought than most men his age; at thirty-six, Margery was as energetic and enthusiastic as a woman in her twenties. Both continued working; they shared housekeeping responsibilities. Earning and sharing, Dell believed, was a "solution of the problems of young love in our present society." The arrangement made him an ardent feminist.

With such differing backgrounds, adjustments were inevitable. Margery's gracious and bookish family life in Evanston and her scholarship to Vassar contrasted with Dell's neglect of manners and scant enjoyment of the ordinary affairs of life. The independent and somewhat bumptious Floyd was, as he writes, "grateful to be humanized by my wife."[7] Actually, the marriage went well; and Dell was happier than he had thought he could be. When, on a trip to Davenport, the Dells found Mollie and George Cook on the point of separation, Dell was disturbed. The Cooks had one child, another on the way, and he thought that, in similar circumstance, he could not have left. For a

Bohemian, his attitudes were strikingly middle class.

Happily settled in their apartment in the Rogers Park district on the near North Side, a location convenient for Margery's teaching in Evanston and Dell's editing at the *Post,* their place soon became a gay and lively center for a group of artists that included the writer Eunice Tietjens; theater director Maurice Browne; Vachel Lindsay; Margaret Anderson, still literary editor of a religious journal; and Margery's father, J. Seymour Currey, the historian. With her charming gifts as hostess, Margery was able to create "an atmosphere in which ideas could dance and sparkle."[8] Dell's capacity for conversation and debate, as well as his position on the *Review,* made him a central figure in the new intellectual and literary excitement of the day. Sometimes parties were held in studios like that of Martha Baker, the miniaturist, who had painted the Dells nude but had added Paris instead of Chicago to the signature. Dell was to make use of the whole episode much later in *Diana Stair* What were mostly the interests, the inclinations, the entertainments of the group were also making history: the so-called Chicago renaissance of arts was underway.

There were problems. Neither Dell's attitudes nor his actions were popular with all. At a time when most Americans—including artists—were fairly reticent about many things, he was perhaps forcing issues as if unaware, really, that conventions even existed. With a fine regard for the truth as he saw it, he spoke and wrote, as a contemporary has observed, with a "youthful insensitiveness to other people's feelings." Some regarded him "as a highly offensive personage whose brilliancy only increased his objectionableness."[9] Because he talked, wrote, and lived according to his own will, he impressed people as being "rude, insulting, egotistic, unprincipled, and dangerous." He was really quite natural, a bit naive; but his intention seemed to be not to shock the bourgeoisie so much as "to let the bourgeoisie know that its ideas profoundly shocked him." His delight and his duty were to make his truths manifest.[10]

Since Dell often acted in unorthodox ways, his comments were thought to be unorthodox also. But his actions were intentional, and his intellectual curiosities, sincere and even orthodox, remained devoted both to abstract beauty and to "a strangely utilitarian kind of social idealism." As he recalled later, "we pretended to a sophistication which we did not possess. We had the air of omniscience. People were always surprised, when they met us, to find how young we were."[11] Whatever his personal whims and conflicts, Dell had become and would remain a significant voice in the literary life of America.

IV *Editor of the* Review

As nearly every critic has observed, the *Friday Literary Review* had been the first to give explanation and documentation to the "newer spirit" of dissent and liberation that was breaking the established bounds of convention. When Dell became editor for the July 28, 1911, issue, it had already become a guide to and a pathfinder for the revolution in literary taste. As editor, Dell made no change in policy: "the standards for which the *Review* has been known in the past will be steadfastly maintained," he wrote; and they were. George Cook, in Chicago and working on a dictionary, joined Dell as associate editor, and remained so even after leaving Chicago the next year; he contributed the "New York Letter" from New York. On October 18, 1912, Lucian Cary was listed as a second associate editor.

Under Dell's direction, a few minor changes may have given the makeup, even the contents, more variety. There is apparent emphasis on American writing, perhaps a warmer sympathy and understanding throughout. The editorials under Dell, shorter but with more variety than those under Hackett, remain vibrant and insurgent. Dell's sentences are not as concise as Hackett's, but he writes with sense and humor. One editorial praises the thousands of young men and women interested in literature: "If it is not theirs to speak, it will be theirs to listen and understand." Another points out the "essential charm" of the secondhand bookstore; one calls attention to American novelists, who, "after the dozen Englishmen of real importance," "demand our appreciation"; one disparages Yeats's "fear of science" as being in a "long line of poets who have expressed in one form or another their dislike and fear of knowledge, of intellect. . . ." Another declares that the unity of criticism lies in taste, "the instinct in the critic that calls to the instinct in the reader." The "most valuable criticism will probably be that which concerns itself instinctively with the intention and methods of the writer. . . ."

Another editorial, which discusses the novel, urges novelists to avoid using "stunts" in description, conversation, psychology, and to give, like Fielding, a "direct revelation of the author's views about people and things." The "peculiar effects of the novel are gained through the continuous imaginative contact *in time* with the characters. . . ." One column praises the "rebel": "merely a citizen of a world which has not yet come into being —a denizen among us, holding our law as lightly, and contemptuous of our good opinions, since we are after all but outlanders." There are other editorials on the writings of Blake and Milton, Donne and Browning. Collectively, the editorials and reviews enunciate Dell's credo.

During his two years as book reviewer under the editorship of Hackett, Dell had already established his own directions. He read each book in question against its social and historical context: he looked for the "genuinely conceived" as against the "merely echoed." He chided William Winter for having "ribald scorn for genius, while so passionately admiring mediocrity." He praised Dostoevsky's "penetrant knowledge" and Belloc's writing for "penetrating to the heart of the commonplace and discovering its secret, its informing mystery." He upheld the literature that gave "the impression of reality," the "real insight into human nature." But he did not settle for mere reporting: in "portraying things as they are," a writer need not give up "a splendid vision of things as they should be." Although the reviews tend to become more and more personal, they lose neither their analytical approach nor their historical perspective.

Some of Dell's finest reviews appear just after he became editor. The one on George Moore's *The Apostle* shows both Dell's method and his skill in handling material: Moore had portrayed Jesus as not dying on the cross but as succumbing to a cataleptic swoon and as meeting Paul later in a monastery. Dell relates Moore's interpretation to myth, which he defines as "ever susceptible to new and vitalizing treatment," and compares Moore's use of it to that of Shakespeare, Milton, Shelley, Browning, and the new poet Ezra Pound. In another review, he defends Mark

Twain as being among "less than half a dozen great writers" in America. Twain, regarded by many as a mere funny man, "knew American life and could write about it like a master. . . ."

Dell also called attention to new poets and to the new continental dramatists; he reviewed sympathetically new books on love and marriage, woman's rights, and socialism. During 1912 he contributed two series: one of these, "Chicago in Fiction," which was composed of eight essays by Dell and one by Cook, focused attention on the city and its writers, including Henry Fuller, Robert Herrick, Theodore Dreiser, Frank Norris, and others. Dell praised the vitality of the city, pointed out literary landmarks, and discussed the new critical spirit that had come to prevail. The six essays in the second series, "Modern Women," confirmed Dell's interest in feminism and furnished material for his first book. Work on the *Review* had given him a reputation as an editor and critic.

V *Around 1912*

The year 1912 "was a beautiful year," Dell said, "a year of poetry, and dreams, and of life renewed and abundant. We were all full of ideals, illusions, and high spirits. We were young, and the world was before us."[12] In May, 1912, he spoke at the centenary celebration of Browning's birth. He contributed two essays—"The Railroad Riots of 1877" and "Socialism and Anarchism in Chicago"—to the five-volume *Chicago: Its History and Its Builders,* which Margery's father was compiling. Under Dell's editorship, the *Review* was, if anything, more brilliant than ever. Dell's knack for knowing writers and good writing enabled him to spot new talent and experimentation. He set up training conferences for book reviewers and gave them instruction: "Bring to bear upon the book, in aesthetic terms, your attitude toward life."[13] Many of these writers were to become well known: Fanny Butcher as literary editor of the Chicago *Tribune*; Llewellyn Jones as literary editor on the *Post*; Margaret Anderson as editor of *The Little Review.*

There were other aspects to the job of editing. In the autumn of 1911, Dell and Margery made their first trip to the publishing houses in New York to see the new books and to meet writers and publishers. Dell's friend Edna Kenton, now in New York, had arranged a meeting with Dreiser, whose *Jennie Gerhardt* Dell had praised in his review. He first met Arnold Bennett in New York at a luncheon, and then again in Chicago, when Bennett talked about writing and growing up in small towns (see Chapter 4). Moreover, in his editorial position, writers often sent him manuscripts, asking for help and criticism. Sometimes, when they came in person, there were long talks either in the office or in a nearby cafe.

And there were other interesting activities and developments. Near the end of 1911 The Abbey Players had performed Synge's plays in Chicago and had inspired Maurice Browne to found the Little Theatre the following year. Dell had supported both ventures in pages of the *Review*; and, as the second project got underway with Brör Nordfeldt doing the scenery for some of the productions, the Little Theatre presented the plays of Wilde and Shaw, of Yeats and Euripides. When Elaine Hyman (Kirah Markham) appeared in the cast of *The Trojan Women,* Dell became infatuated with her. After a while, she turned to Theodore Dreiser, who had arrived in Chicago just before the year's end. For nearly two months Dreiser was an active and invigorating figure in the literary life of the city, being honored by Maurice Browne and praised by Dell.

In August, 1912, when Harriet Monroe sent her "poet's circular" letter to writers in America and Britain, Dell had received one and called her idea "an exciting event—my interest grows by leaps and bounds."[14] The first issues of *Poetry,* dated October, 1912, appeared in late September to make literary history. In March, 1913, when part of the New York Armory Show came to Chicago and was attacked by "philistines," Dell, Browne, and others came to its defense. The year 1912 had been significant for both Dell and Chicago, but events in Dell's personal life were already working toward profound changes for his future.

VI   *The Young Bohemians*

"With the arrival of the Dells" in the Jackson Park area on the near South Side, "Chicago bohemia," writes Dale Kramer,

"had come into its own."[15] The temporary structures, built at
the time of the World's Fair as little shops, had become studios
where artists and writers lived in sometimes primitive but inex-
pensive quarters. In April, 1913, when two studios became va-
cant, the Dells moved from their Rogers Park apartment.
Margery took the more luxurious studio—it had a bathtub—on
Stony Island Avenue; Dell, the one on Fifty-seventh Street. The
arrangement was convenient; their back doors nearly touched.

The painter Brör Nordfeldt occupied the corner studio between the Dells; it was Nordfeldt who painted Dell as the young
Bohemian with high collar and stock. The portrait, which surely
helped to establish Dell's reputation and identity as the arch-
Bohemian, had caused him to write the story, "The Portrait of
Murray Swift," in which he views and criticizes himself. Kath-
leen Wheeler, a sculptress; Marjorie Jones, photographer and
friend; and Raymond Johnson and Lou Wall Moore of the
Little Theatre lived in nearby studios.

And, with Margery as hostess, the Dells continued to enter-
tain. They were a living example of companionate marriage.
Sherwood Anderson and Carl Sandburg brought to their home
manuscripts; later Dell would assist Anderson in his writing career. At one party, Margaret Anderson announced plans for her
new magazine, *The Little Review.* Arthur Davison Ficke came,
as did Charles Hallinan, Lucian Cary, and others. In *The Briary-
Bush,* Dell re-created the joy and spirit of this period in his life,
which had been relatively brief, yet had contained both public
success and personal failure.

Whatever the outward appearances, the move to separate studios signified that something in Dell's marriage had gone wrong;
something had, and the fault was probably his. Partly, he had
only begun to put in practice the ideas of "free love" that everyone had been talking about. As he writes in *Homecoming,*
"there was a girl; and we kissed." He told Emily Hahn, "I started
drifting around, falling in love with other women, and the end
was inevitable."[16] His old world, once real enough, seemed now
but a shadow; in this new world he felt free and happy—"like a
wanderer long absent in alien lands, who sets eyes again upon
his native place." In coming to that place—not unlike a homecoming—he felt truly himself putting forth "no effort . . . to be

what one was not. . . ."[17] Dell, who had believed in the reality
of custom and habit, now found that a stolen and illicit love
meant much, that in this private dream world he might take his
ease. When he tried to give up his new freedom, he only fell in
love again. There was a rush of creative writing, as if he could
"disguise the characters, and get it off my mind."

Although he did not—could not—believe that his marriage was
shattered, Margery knew that the end had come; she could only
wait for his realization. Her letter wishing him "all the joy and
completeness you'll one day know and which I'll dream of for
you" has all the strength of her generous personality.[18] As
Dell says

I don't think any of us quite knew what we believed about love and "freedom." We were in love with life, and willing to believe almost any modern
thing which gave us a chance to live our lives more fully. We were incredi-
bly well meaning. We were confused, miserable, gay, and robustly happy,
all at once. . . . We were intensely alive; we inflicted blind unintentional
cruelties upon those we loved, but there was no meanness and no cynicism
in our hearts; and there was beauty, and trust, and candor, and forgiveness.[19]

A conflict in Dell remained, perhaps forever irreconcilable: an
obligation to order and custom, yet an impulse to rebel against
those very rules that circumscribe and warp man's natural impulse. He was, however, beginning to see that out of pain and
suffering came joy and wisdom, and that an individual must
learn to adapt himself to the thoughts and feelings and lives of
others, as well as to a rapidly changing machine culture. This
indelible lesson stimulated much of his finest writing.

Partly because of Dell's modern attitudes and liberal ideas,
the *Friday Literary Review* was suspended with the April 25th,
1913, issue as a separate publication and became only pages in
the *Post*. Then, in September, while on the publishers' rounds in
New York, Dell learned that several editors on the *Post* had
been fired; he wired his own resignation and returned to Chicago
only to wind up his affairs. There were, doubtless, many reasons
for his action. As Kramer points out, he was, perhaps, a little
weary of outwitting the editors of the *Post*; perhaps he was
tired of what had become a routine job and of writing mostly
about what others had written; perhaps his sense of fun and

creativity had vanished; and surely an awareness of his own emotional nature had left him a little bewildered and uncertain. To others, Dell seemed the archetypal Bohemian of the Nordfeldt portrait—shy, arrogant, a little dangerous; and his bold ideas and cruel wit made him seem all that was "inspiriting or alarming."

In any event, Chicago, as Harry Hansen has said, has often been but "a way station," where passengers alighted and then went on. At the age of twenty-six, Dell had become recognized and respected there as a literary critic, editor, and essayist. His had been a liberating voice in a world where literary Realism and experimentation with form were still not wholly accepted. He had been a pioneer in thought and ideas; and, if he had helped others, he had, despite the outcome of his marriage, learned something about himself, something about the necessity of being more human. He had not yet learned to cope fully with his emotional life, but he clearly saw that he could not do so in Chicago. Margery had already accepted a job with the Chicago *Daily News.* In November, 1913, Dell boarded the train for New York.

VII   Women as World Builders

Women as World Builders appeared in the summer of 1913. Dell's first volume was composed of essays which had already been published in the *Friday Literary Review* about ten feminist leaders. His interest in feminism—aided, doubtless, by Margery's work in the suffragette movement—had mostly derived from his own "somewhat utopian conception of working-class revolution." Both in theory and in fact, he admired women's ability and believed that they should be free to develop their own individuality. He wanted them to be equals, even comrades of men; and he hoped that they could and would achieve such status. He said later that this book enabled him to work a compromise between his own "narcistic [*sic*] impulses and the sexual-social impulses," and that here his narcissistic tendencies were given free outlet in a kind of realistic utopianism in which women are "free to pursue their own self-chosen creative tasks."[20] Indeed, he saw that their freedom was also part of his own demands and desires for freedom.

Dell's concern in *Women as World Builders* is with woman as producer, not with woman as lover; but he recognizes that she may be both and lauds her aspiration. Nor is he concerned with woman-worship—"for woman as virgin, or wife, or mother, irrespective of her capacities as friend or leader or servant—that is Romance"; but he had no intention of robbing women of their charm and strength and beauty (17). Nor has he included a discussion of woman and sex: "The adjustment of one's social and personal relations, so far as may be, to accord with one's own convictions—that is not feminism, in my opinion: it is only common sense" (9). Relying on sociology, on the study of women's possibilities, he sets out to understand their "essential nature" and to show "what may be expected from a future in which women will have a larger freedom and a larger influence" (76).

To show the Feminist movement in its many aspects—woman as economist, as politician, as worker, dancer, statistician, labor organizer—Dell examines the careers of individual, and exceptional, women; he does not treat the subject as sociological abstraction, for he wanted to preserve the "personal tone and color," which, he believed, was the "life of any movement" (7). The ten Feminist leaders included Charlotte Perkins Gilman, editor and publisher, poet, economist; Jane Addams, reformer and sociologist, founder of Hull House; Mrs. Emmeline Pankhurst, suffragette leader; Olive Schreiner, economist and author, whose *Women and Labor* argues for women's freedom to work; Isadora Duncan, artist and dancer, who created a renaissance in the freedom of bodily expression; Beatrice Potter Webb, statistician and Fabian Socialist; Emma Goldman, anarchist, editor (*Mother Earth*), pacifist; Margaret Dreir Robins, economist and leader in the Women's Trade Union League; Ellen Key, sociologist and writer, whose *Love and Marriage* advocates a freedom in morality that includes trial marriage, the beauty of love and motherhood, whether sanctioned by the law or not; and Dora Marsden, British editor of *The Freewoman,* who propagandized for women and attacked all things that thwarted woman's freedom. In statements that were radical for 1913, Dell concludes that "women have a surer instinct than men for the preservation of the truest human values" and that their "acts of conservatism will seem to the timid minds among us like . . . the debacle of civilization. . . ." (89)

The essays in Dell's first volume recorded what was to be a lifelong interest in the Feminist movement, as well as his interest in the psychology of women and in the necessity for them—as for men—to adapt to a modern machine culture. Here, and in the reviews, he had given expression to ideas and themes that were to emerge in short stories and poetry and plays, and later in novels and in studies of love and marriage.

Dell's stay in Chicago had netted more intellectual achievement than emotional satisfaction. If Dell were a little bewildered, he left Chicago still believing in love and marriage, and still optimistic about his emotional future. He had changed; he had become, he said, more human. He had learned something about freedom and love, something about himself and the ordinary affairs of life. But there were uncertainties; there were conclusions still to be reached. As he says, it "would take years to find out" the lessons that he had learned.

CHAPTER 3

Dell in New York

THE CHICAGO YEARS had established Dell as a hard-working and talented editor of an important literary review, who had been a leader and liberating influence in the "Chicago renaissance"; and the sojourn in New York and Croton-on-Hudson, which lasted until the mid-1930's, brought success and recognition not only as reviewer and editor but also as a critic and novelist. His stay was partly the logical achievement of ideals that had made the Chicago years seem unfulfilled. The young Dell who set out to work in Greenwich Village had already abandoned his high collar and black stock for a blue flannel shirt; and, while life in the Village was joyous and exciting, Dell was working very hard: in addition to writing poems, stories, plays, and versions of a novel, he was doing editorial chores first on *The Masses* and then on *The Liberator.* There was, of course, time for parties and conversations and love affairs; to some, Dell appeared as the prototype of the Greenwich Villager. But the adventures in sex, the readings in psychology, and the trips to the psychoanalyst were helping him to understand his relation to others, to self, to a changing world. The sojourn in New York was, therefore, formative and decisive.

Dell already knew something of the Village when he arrived there in the autumn of 1913, but what he was about to witness was not just another year in its history, but the birth of a new Village—the one he called the "Seventh," which had begun to appear around 1911. In general, as Daniel Aaron points out, the young intellectuals who came there had not only inherited a traditional culture against which they were rebelling but lived at a "time of general economic and social stability"; like the young hopefuls of Emerson's day, they rebelled but had not lost touch with traditional values. As Dell wrote in 1921, "They were engaged in trying to see the world anew—to see in imagination, and

with the help of reason, what it might become."[1] They had
grown up in towns and villages; they had read Emerson and
Whitman, Thoreau, Jefferson, Rousseau; in their "intellectual
vagabondage," they had been enthusiastic about Ibsen, Nietzsche,
Marx, Wells, Shaw, Freud. And, while they criticized and rebelled and attacked repression and bigotry in economics, art, religion, education, and sex, they did not, as a newer generation
of Villagers would shortly do, "reject completely the entire bat-
tery of cultural, political, and economic assumptions that had
sustained an older America."[2]

Although the Village was a definite place, in another sense, as
Hippolyte Havel observed, "Greenwich Village is a state of
mind, it has no boundaries."[3] Art Young remembers it as "the
old home where once a band of neophytes from the monastery
of custom started something–different."[4] As Dell wrote in
1933, the Village meant many things: it was a place where rents
were cheap, where people were free to be themselves, where
they came to solve their problems–a kind of "moral-health resort," where they found peace and tolerance, a refuge from
middle-class morality, especially the attitude toward sex.[5] For
many, of course, the Village was simply home, a place where
work was done, where life was lived freely, creatively, but in-
dustriously. Gay, yet serious, many Villagers were, as Dell said,
"pilgrims on an unknown pilgrimage," ". . . seeking understanding of themselves and of the mysteries of life."[6] There where a
"tangle of crooked little streets shut out the tide of traffic, and
left a quiet island," life was "the play of artists, simple and in-
genuous; the talk was golden, and the loves were frank and
candid."[7]

While living on the south side of Washington Square, Dell be-
gan looking for a job. While looking, he wrote and sold a few
stories and began to make more friends–he already knew Arthur
Ficke, George Cook, Susan Glaspell, who were now in New
York. Within a day or so after his arrival, Henrietta Rodman,
who would play a prominent role in the new Village, had asked
him to write a play for the Liberal Club's opening. One noon in
December, Dell was walking past Gallup's Restaurant, where
Max Eastman and other *Masses* editors were having lunch.
Berkeley Tobey, the business manager for the magazine, spotted
him. As Eastman recalls, "Tobey said: 'There goes your associate

editor—that's Floyd Dell!' "[8] Horatio Winslow, a writer for *Puck,* rushed out to Dell and led him back to Gallup's. John Reed, who would be leaving shortly for Mexico, told him: "Floyd, you are going to help edit the *Masses.* You know about make-up and such things. You will attend to all that, while Max writes the editorials. Your title will be associate editor."[9] Dell accepted their offer of twenty-five dollars a week, but on one condition; for, as he told them,

. . Bohemian ways are all right in some respects, but not, in my view, when it comes to money matters. I know how it is over at the *Masses'* office. Sometimes the office force doesn't get paid because there isn't any money. But I expect to be paid whether there is any money or not. The first time I don't get paid, I won't say anything. The next time I don't get paid, I won't say anything, either, but I won't be there any more.[10]

Eastman, who was on the point of resigning, wrote later that Dell's arrival saved the magazine: "I never knew a more reasonable or dependable person, more variously intelligent, more agile in combining sociability with industry, and I never knew a writer who had his talents in such complete command."[11]

I   The Masses

The Masses was then and remains one of the few exciting magazines published in the twentieth century. Founded in January, 1911, by Piet Vlag "to help improve the conditions of the working people, *'whether they want it or not,'* "[12] *The Masses* had run into financial difficulty by the autumn of 1912. It was then that the contributors elected Max Eastman, recently ousted from teaching at Columbia University for outspoken opinions on social conflict, as editor of the magazine—without pay. As editor, Eastman made the magazine a unique venture: he "wanted everybody to express his own individuality to the limit [and everybody did], so long as he did not transgress the principles of socialism."[13] Using suggestions from John Reed, Eastman composed his own statement of aims, first used as an appeal to subscribers, and later run permanently with the masthead:

This Magazine is Owned and Published Co-operatively by its Editors. It has no Dividends to Pay, and nobody is trying to make Money out of it. A Revolutionary and not a Reform Magazine; a Magazine with a sense of Humor and no Respect for the Respectable; Frank; Arrogant; Impertinent;

Searching for the True Causes; a Magazine Directed against Rigidity and Dogma wherever it is found; Printing what is too Naked or True for a Money-making Press; a Magazine whose final Policy is to do as it Pleases and Conciliate Nobody, not even its Readers—there is a Field for this Publication in America.[14]

Socialist in direction, but against the rabid devotee and the smart-alecky leftist, anti-Bohemian in tenor, anticlerical, and, much of the time, antiwar, *The Masses* joined "in the struggle for racial equality and woman's rights, for intelligent sex relations above all (and beneath all) for birth and population control."[15] In art and literature, *The Masses* tended toward Realism. As Dell wrote in a letter to Arthur Ficke, "I believe The Masses has the opinion of itself that it cannot be shocked: I know better. And you know that poor old Floyd, with his classical standards still fluttering in the cyclone of modernism, is very capable of it. . . ."[16] With liberty as the goal of the class struggle, the magazine emphasized the ideal "that every individual should be made free to live and grow in his own chosen way."[17] For Dell, *The Masses* "stood for fun, truth, beauty, realism, freedom, peace, feminism, revolution."[18]

As managing editor, Dell spent much of his time in *The Masses* office and bookstore on Greenwich Avenue. He was "keeper of the manuscripts," the one who returned them to the sender with a "Sorry, F. D." Often dressed in his white pants, his Byronic collar, and his orange-colored tie, he also presided at the monthly meetings, those hilarious sessions of fun and seriousness, where in some artist's studio—"up several flights of stairs"—the editors assembled to select material for the next issue. In an "atmosphere of dreamy adventure," Art Young remembers, "we were sailing out, so to speak, with no chart but our untried beliefs and a kind of confidence that any way might be better than the old way."[19] Here they discussed and voted on stories, poems, pictures, essays; even visitors came, participated in the discussions, voted.

Dell recalls that "brilliant speeches of criticism" often swayed the vote; but, in the end, although he and Eastman had a portfolio of half-approved and sometimes useful material, they had to gather or write new material. Eastman and Dell worked well together, bringing out a magazine that mingled the arty and the satiric, the comic and the serious. Dorothy Day, assistant managing editor for a while, remembers that Dell demanded near perfection in articles and reviews, recalls his revisions of "sentences and even entire paragraphs neatly rewritten in bright green ink, the handwriting so plain that the copy can go to the printer as it is."[20] With Dell on the staff, "the magazine took on a fuller literary flavor." Many of his contemporaries agreed with Paul Jordan-Smith that Floyd Dell was "the greatest book-reviewer in the world."[21]

Dell also contributed articles, short stories, and poems to *The Masses.* One of his stories, "The Beating," about the treatment of a young girl in a reform school, had a startling illustration by John Sloan. Dell wrote about birth control, burlesque, cartoons, the chances of peace, conscientious objectors, and Feminism. The book reviews that he continued to write had a gay and personal touch, but he could also relate a book to past ideas and tradition, to present thought and event. His reviews, enjoyable and informative, made the reader want to examine that book for himself.

Dell's zest for discovering the truth and writing about it with wit, irony, and candor also gave the reviews a breadth and depth of insight. He subscribed to the magazine's policy of Realism and revolution, but he maintains his own point of view with its mixture of idealism and reason. His objective treatment of his material makes for analysis rather than mere praise or blame. Committed in general to the new Realistic directions in literature with such literary heroes as Shaw and Wells, Dell continues to admire, not the Dreiser who never laughs, but the Dreiser who, with the strange, fascinating beauty, is true to life.

He praises the "gift of truth-telling" of Russian writers—truths that will survive "revolution or reaction, communism or capitalism"—and their gift of candor and "self-revelation," which "English prose literature has always very sadly lacked." He deplores the tiresomeness of "sociological generalizations" in fiction, and the pleasure of getting "down to the romantic, un-modern, eternally fascinating facts of human nature"; he praises Conrad's ability to present "romance in the most realistic terms—fantasy solid as birches; beautiful and wonderful and tragic dreams that seem more true than waking life. . . ." He says that a review of a novel ought to contain "a history of English fiction," and in reviewing Gilbert Cannan's *Mendel,* he illustrates with a thumbnail sketch from the first thriller, *Beowulf,* through the stories of Chaucer, the sociological study that is *Piers Plowman,* the psychological studies of Shakespeare and Dostoevsky and James, the satire of Fielding, and "the failure of the Antimacassar or Victorian Age to contribute anything but impedimenta to its development. . . ." He is sometimes cordial, sometimes antagonistic to experimenters, to the "art-for-art's sake" school, the Dadaists, the Surrealists.

Many readers enjoyed Dell's writing because it combined a hope of revolution with an appreciation of artistry and beauty. He had, with his candor and truth-telling and sharply incisive humor, helped to create a magazine that he has described as "unique in the history of journalism, a magazine of our own in which we could say what we thought about everything in the world."[22] He wrote: "We did not agree with other people about a lot of things. We did not agree with each other about many things. We were fully agreed only upon one point, that it was a jolly thing to have a magazine in which we could freely express our individual thoughts and feelings in stories and poems and pictures and articles and jokes."[23] Of the Village magazines at that time, *The Masses* was, as Albert Parry writes, "the earliest of them, also the most lasting, also of the most telling force and influence."[24]

II   *The Young Villager*

"Rents were low in Greenwich Village; that was why artists and writers lived there," Dell wrote in 1947. He remembered the Village of pre-World War I as a hospitable place for sensitive and serious men and women. Most of them were young; few had money; only some had real talent. University people, students, professors, social workers, writers, and artists, they "paid their bills and bathed regularly." Dell thought they were a "superior lot of people," who had "most of the familiar middle-class virtues, and in addition some of their own."[25] If they came for economic reasons, they surely stayed for the sheer joy of living there.

The social center of the Village was the Liberal Club, which had, when Dell arrived, just moved into quarters above Polly's newly opened restaurant on Macdougal Street. The club's guiding spirit was Henrietta Rodman, a high-school teacher, protester, and blazer of trails, whom Dell called Egeria in *Love in Greenwich Village.* As he said, "She invented Greenwich Village—the Greenwich Village whose gay laughter was heard around the world."[26] When she asked Dell to write a play for the opening of the club, he and Arthur Ficke invented a plot about Saint George in Greenwich Village, which, as Dell recalls, "made fun of our earnest modernity." The play's success not only helped the popularity of the club, but gave Dell the first of many opportunities to write one-act plays and sometimes to perform in them.

In 1916 when George Cram Cook brought the Provincetown Players to a brownstone house in the Village, Dell's *King Arthur's Socks,* along with several other plays, was on the first bill. It was during readings of his *The Angel Intrudes* that Edna St. Vincent Millay, newly arrived in the Village, appeared and tried out for the role of Annabelle. Since playwrights were in charge of direction, Dell was there himself for the tryout. She was given the part, but it was later that Dell fell in love with her. Although the war had come and time was surely changing the world, the years were also making "improbable and delightful things" happen. Life in the Village had its own charm; there were girls to meet; and, if enough money, dinner at the Brevoort; and sometimes masquerade balls. Or one could meet friends at the Working Girls' Home or at Polly's for a drink and talk. As Dell recalls, "I was a Villager . . . in the time before the invasion of the barbarians from Uptown, before Pepe raised the rents—the Golden Age."[27]

But a golden age may lose its lustre. As Dell writes, "if there had been no girls in Greenwich Village I could have lived there almost as inexpensively as Thoreau did in his cabin on Walden Pond."[28] But there were many girls, and Dell has told how a man and a girl could share a flat, with his and her name on the door. His own love affair had ended after two years and was followed by a succession of others. There were emotional upsets. Sometimes friends did not welcome a new sweetheart. Loyalties and snobberies continued to exist even in the free-loving Village.

With the new generation that began to appear around 1916, Dell and others were looked on as conservative; and, in part, he had always been so. As he began to take stock of his emotional responses, he saw that some of his theories (and practices) seemed no longer true. There were consequences and limits to freedom. With his creed already formulated "around Socialism and revolution," he did not seek a new one. Instead, he wanted "continuity and stability" in both his work and life; and, whatever his Bohemian habits, he continued to think in terms of a wife and family: ". . . I wanted to be father to any children I had, not a romantic begetter who proceeded to wander away over the face of the earth in pursuit of some new illusion."[29] A decade later his novels *Runaway* and *An Unmarried Father* reflect the clash of feelings that he had experienced.

Like many Villagers whose background was that of "unimpeachable respectability," Dell began to realize that he had, perhaps, never fully accepted the role of lover, Bohemian, and vagabond which he had, in part, been playing. But he also saw that appeals to self-sacrifice, to alcohol, to utopian theories would neither expiate the guilt nor serve as happy escapes. Nor did he want to think of life as having been a mere collection of brief love affairs, little partings, divorces. At the same time his accomplishments in work—the book-reviewing, editing, writing—were not wholly satisfying. For a while he lived in New Jersey, then moved from one part of the Village to another, from one affair to another. By 1916 his divorce from Margery Currey had become legal. At the age of thirty, he had not come fully to terms with himself. He might well have asked if he had mistaken change for growth and a role or personae for reality.

Because of this concern for self, this desire to "succeed" in finishing his novel, this hope to improve his character, this feeling of need at his age to stay in love with the same girl, Dell went to a psychoanalyst in the late months of 1917 and on into 1918. As he has said, "I wanted to be set free to love deeply enough to get married and have children; and I wanted to find in myself the powers necessary for completing my novel."[30] The analysis and talks with Dr. S. A. Tannenbaum, to whom he later dedicated *The Briary-Bush,* helped him to gain a deeper insight into himself and into the world. He became an early supporter of the methods of the psychoanalyst for certain kinds of treatment; although he did not feel that such methods could supplant the Socialist's analysis of life, he firmly believed that psychological analysis could unearth infor nation that could be had by no other means: it could afford truths that made the "dying old world" seem young. With a clearer grasp of the relation of youth and idealism to the process of growing up, and with a firmer understanding of the necessity of adapting himself to life as it is, the writer and idealist, the Puritan, the Socialist, the psychologist began to see his novel take satisfactory form. But now there were other problems, public ones that had to be considered out of necessity, not choice.

III   The Masses *Trials*

The second decade of the twentieth century was an era of turbulence and change that culminated in World War I. Problems with Cuba, the Philippines, Panama, Japan, Mexico, and Latin America had involved the United States more and more in international affairs until a complexity of issues led the nation into the European conflict. Although 1912 is now known as the "Lyric year" of poetry and although 1913 brought the great Armory art show, the decade was one of strife and agitation for needed social and political reform. In 1913, following the strike in Paterson, New Jersey, John Reed had organized the famous pageant that was held in Madison Square Garden; in 1914, the Ludlow Massacre at a Colorado mining camp had horrified the nation. Max Eastman, who had gone there, had reported his findings in *The Masses*; and the magazine, sometimes echoing attacks made by an older muckraking era, spoke out for birth control; for woman's rights and suffrage; for social justice to workers, Negroes, and strikers; for neutrality and nonintervention in the European war. Although some of the editors—Dell was one—did not continue their opposition to the war, the magazine continued to criticize war and war profiteering, to defend pacifists and conscientious objectors, and to oppose the ferocity of government action against minority opinion under the Espionage Act.[31]

Even before its August, 1917, issue was barred from the mails and the editors were indicted for conspiracy, *The Masses* had had difficulties over "truth-telling." In 1913, Eastman and Art Young had been indicted for charging the Associated Press "with having suppressed and colored the news" in reporting a strike in West Virginia. In 1916, John S. Sumner, Anthony Comstock's successor as secretary of the Society for the Suppression of Vice, confiscated the September issue and arrested Merrill Rogers, business manager, for the reason "that we had advertised and sold 'The Sexual Question', by August Forel. . . ."

But the real difficulty came after Congress passed the Espionage Act, and Wilson signed it into law on June 15, 1917. The law provided up to twenty years imprisonment and/or a fine up to $10,000 for persons who willfully made false reports to help the enemy, who incited rebellion among the armed forces, or who attempted to obstruct recruiting or the operation of the draft. The postmaster general was empowered to deny the use of the mails to any material which, in his opinion, advocated treason, insurrection, or forcible resistance to the laws of the United States. On July 3, the August issue of *The Masses* was presented for mailing at the New York post office; but at a conference of the solicitor of the Post Office, the attorney general, and judge advocate general of the army, the decision was made to exclude it from the mails. Specifically, four cartoons and four passages of text, including the unsigned piece by Dell on conscientious objectors, were cited as violations of the law. Although Judge Learned Hand declared the case free of the charge, the New York postmaster appealed the decision to a higher court, and a stay of execution of Judge Hand's order was given. When the September issue was presented to the post office, the mailing privilege was not restored to the magazine on the grounds that, since the August issue had not been mailed, the magazine was an irregular publication.

During the time that Eastman was working on the case, Dell and his assistant continued to assemble the magazine from "material voluntarily submitted by the contributing editors." The magazine came out, but the October and a November–December issue were sold only on news stands. The end had come: *The Masses* office was closed in November, 1917. Although still under indictment, Eastman began to plan almost at once for a new magazine; but, because of continued attempts to have *The Masses* charges dropped, it was March before *The Liberator,* reviving a name that William Lloyd Garrison had made famous, began publication, with Eastman and his sister as joint editors and with Dell as associate editor.

Eastman and Dell were in reality supporting the President and the war effort when the first *Masses* trial got underway on April 15, 1918. Serious as the trial was, an account of it now seems ludicrous, a kind of grim joke. As Dell has written, it was like "a scene from 'Alice in Wonderland' rewritten by Dostoievsky." The case against Josephine Bell, a poet in no way connected with the magazine, was dismissed at once. Reed was still in Russia; H. J. Glintenkamp had gone to Mexico; Eastman, Dell, Art Young, and Merrill Rogers, the business manager, stood trial. Augustus N. Hand was on the bench; Morris Hillquit, a recent Socialist candidate for mayor of New York, and Dudley Field Malone, who had resigned as collector of the Port of New York, defended them; and Assistant District Attorney Earl B. Barnes was in charge of the prosecution. The charge of conspiring to cause mutiny and refusing to do duty in the armed forces was thrown out. The four men, as well as the Masses Publishing Company, were thus tried for conspiring to "obstruct recruiting and enlistment to the injury of the service."

Just outside the old Post Office Building, where the windows of the courtroom looked down on a Liberty Bond booth and a rally in progress, a brass band struck up the national anthem—as it did every few hours. Each time, Merrill Rogers sprang to attention, with the others following, and finally the whole courtroom, until, at last, the judge had to dispense with such ceremony. Once Art Young fell asleep and, when awakened, drew his own portrait to illustrate the event. Before the trial had ended, Young and other artists present had sketched nearly everyone.

As intellectuals with verbal gifts, the defendants, especially Eastman and Dell, answered questions and spoke at length with wit and skill. All of them denied that there had been any conspiracy involved, for there had not been. As Art Young writes, "Eastman and Dell tried to make clear that it had never been possible to get all the 'co-operating' editors and contributors together at any one time."[32] How, then, could they have conspired? Friends came to listen; when Eastman spoke, the courtroom was filled.

Dell was the fourth defendant to take the stand. Among his writings, a particular paragraph from his introductory comment to a number of letters from English prisons by conscientious objectors had been cited as overt violation of the act. In part he had written: "There are some laws which the individual feels that he *cannot obey,* and which he will suffer any punishment, even that of death, rather than recognize them as having authority over him. This fundamental stubbornness of the free soul, against which all the powers of the state are helpless, constitutes a conscientious objection, whatever its original sources may be in political or social opinion."[33]

It was not that Dell was opposed to conscription. He explained: "But I want a democratic conscription, a conscription of the willing, again to use a phrase of our President, and I said that any such conscription must be based upon one definite principle: and that is, if there is any person whose conscience will not allow him to take up arms, who could only do it in gross violation of his soul, he should not be compelled to take up arms."[34]

Later, in telling how it felt to be tried, Dell wrote that ". . . I may as well confess that I took it with pleasure. I had always secretly felt that my opinions were of a certain importance. It appeared that the government agreed with me." He had "found in cross-examination the distinct amusement of a primitive sort of game of wits."[35] Dell quickly avoided falling into Attorney Barnes's verbal traps. The prosecutor found that he had correctly described Dell as "a trained journalist, a writer of exquisite English, keenly ironical, bitingly sarcastic."[36]

By April 25, the testimony had been given and the summaries stated; the jury retired; on April 27, still hopelessly deadlocked, the jurors were finally discharged. The defendants were free but still under indictment. Later it was learned that the twelfth juror, a Henry C. Fredericks, had believed in their innocence all along and had even won several others to his side. With the trial over, Dell returned for a while to the more familiar patterns of Village life.

But the war was already bringing changes. Now a major in the army, Arthur Ficke appeared in New York, fell in love with Edna Millay, but soon left for France. Dell and Millay resumed their love affair; then, in the summer, Dell's draft number came up. With strong sympathies for the Allies, he was ready enough to go into uniform. As he wrote in *The Liberator* just before his induction: " . . . I do not wish to discourage the government in its happy ambition of making a soldier out of me. That plan, by its very boldness, commands my respect, and if it proves successful will have my hearty applause."[37] Inducted into the army on June 27, he was sent to Camp Wadsworth near Spartanburg, South Carolina. He was, of course, still under indictment, a fact which had evidently been overlooked. On July 7 he was given a discharge; and, with several days' pay in his pocket, he returned to New York. He found an apartment at 11 Christopher Street and was soon back at the office of *The Liberator.* His series of articles on education began appearing in the magazine in August, 1918. Then, in September, the editors of *The Masses* were brought to trial for the second time.

The first trial had lasted nearly two weeks; the second took less than half that time. With their new attorney and before a new judge, the former defendants were now joined by John Reed, back from Russia. Again the arguments were presented; again Dell explained "in his precise and slightly nervous manner, why he had opposed the war, and exactly what changes in the President's policy had brought him to support it."[38] Again Eastman spoke, defining socialism, pleading for respect of the idea, explaining with dignity and eloquence his position. Again the jury disagreed—eight for acquittal, four for conviction—and once again the trial ended. On January 10, 1919, the indictment was dismissed, and the impounded correspondence was returned to the defendants. As John Reed reported, "it has been said that the disagreement of the jury in this second *Masses* case is a victory for free speech, and for international Socialism. In a way this is true."[39] At any rate, the defendants were free; and Dell once more returned to his chores on *The Liberator.* But, with the end of the war, life in the Village had already changed considerably.

IV   *Decline of the Village*

The excitement that had helped create the Village in 1911 was still strong during the war, but by 1916 the Village which Dell and his friends had known was no longer existent. During and after the war, "uptowners," who had begun to discover it as a place of amusement, invaded the restaurants, and sought the "merry bohemians." Then, as the place began to fall "victim to realtors, showmen, and all manner of tourist-catching allurements," as Art Young recalls, it grew tawdry and commercialized.[40] As prices and rents increased, the older Villagers found new haunts, but these too were soon discovered. The Liberal Club began to lose members and money; Polly's restaurant, no longer serving the club's clientele, moved to a new location. New coteries claimed new places: the Dutch Oven, the Mad Hatter, the Purple Pup.

When the "uptowners" also discovered the Village balls, sponsored once by *The Masses* and now revived by the Liberal Club, the invasion of the balls finished, as Dell put it, "the process which the restaurants had begun."[41] The Village no longer seemed either a retreat or a place in which to work or play. It had become a catch-all, a carnival, a cabaret; in the 1920's it would become a speakeasy. New voices, actively revolutionary and often blatant, like that of Mike Gold, had already appeared in *The Masses* and were continuing in *The Liberator.* The Washington Square Players, later the Theatre Guild, was moving uptown. By 1920, the Provincetown Players had taken O'Neill's *Emperor Jones* to Broadway, and the Cooks had found their way to Greece.

Yet Dell remained in the Village, working hard. If the new "half-Villagers" looked on him as a fallen spokesman and protested what they considered violations of their code, they knew neither Dell nor the Village that he had known and had helped to prosper through social vision and dedication.

V   The Liberator

Although there were to be later changes in editorial policies and in editors, *The Liberator* became a brilliant successor to

The Masses. As Eastman says, it was "less rambunctious," for the editors hoped to avoid trouble with the censor. Owned by Eastman and his sister, it was no longer a cooperative; all contributors were to receive payment. Probably more Socialist than *The Masses,* the magazine stood for the "struggle of labor"; for public ownership of railroads, mines, public utilities; for independence of women; birth control; new methods of education, an end to racial segregation. It was also for the war in Russia and for the war as "expounded by President Wilson." It stood for complete freedom in all the arts.

In addition to Dell's duties as associate editor, he continued to write articles and reviews; and if, to use Daniel Aaron's phrasing, the " 'bourgeois heart' struggled privately with the 'Socialist head'," Dell continued to speak out for revolutionary socialism and, at the same time, to affirm the importance of art and beauty in life as separate from politics, yet related to human endeavor. If he had come to believe that form and order were necessary to his own life, and to his art, and if these were surely traditional, even conservative, in pattern, his findings did not abrogate his continued belief in the need for revolutionary thinking in any and all fields and for the right to assert that belief.

Dell's book reviews and articles in *The Liberator* are as brilliant as anything he was to write. In highly personal terms, he ranges over a number of writers and expresses himself on a variety of subjects: he writes about revolution and politics, freedom and creativity, realism and the craft of writing, dreams and the function of poetry. Specific examples show the shape of his thinking at this time: with near-Emersonian belief in the constant re-examination of ideas, he takes another look at socialism. In commenting on Bertrand Russell's "political ideals," Dell notes that in witnessing the breakup of Socialist certainties himself, he has begun to doubt the effectiveness of a system that might lead only to a servile state. Even in time of war, there is need to reformulate political ideals that will, as Russell sees it, include "the whole world" in a political unity that "neither destroys nor exalts the State" but "will encourage the creative impulses in all mankind" to a "Newer International."

And Dell sees that Chesterton's mode of thought, older than Marxism, "really is *revolutionary* in its essence, which Marxian

or scientific socialism is not." Marx did provide hope for the
working class, but reliance on vast historical processes and fate,
not on personal responsibility, brings spiritual inertia and the
loss of freedom. Action demands "Christian courage and the
faith that is beyond knowledge." The problem lies with the
meaning of determinism and of free will: determinism is true in
the field of knowledge; in the field of action it is "mere mischie-
vous nonsense. After we have acted, we may . . . speculate upon
the natural forces which inevitably determined our action; but
at the moment of action we must conceive ourselves free to
act." If we are to think and to act in revolutionary terms, then
"going back to the path from which we wandered a few hundred years ago may be the most progressive thing to do."

Although Dell rejects nationalism for internationalism—an
"alliance with the workers of the world"—and praises Lenin,
who "talked of work, of discipline, machinery . . . ," as the
"great man of today and tomorrow," he returns, in other reviews, to the link between socialism and poetry that he found in
revolutionary and creative impulses. Reviewing Bertrand Russell's *Proposed Roads to Freedom* in 1919, he castigates "all
forms of organization" that usurp the "first flush of creative enthusiasm." If his aversion may be neurotic, it is also *"artistic"*:
the "revolt of the sensitive and essentially egotistic and solitary
artist, against the timid, stifling, uncomfortable democracy of
the herd." Such a spirit characterizes pioneer and philosopher—
Emerson, Nietzsche, Tolstoy, Thoreau, Whitman. And, while the
spirit is fierce and destructive, it also leavens mankind and "necessarily implies the search for or the creation of an ideal community of free spirits."

In his observations on the novel, Dell praises Dreiser's "zest,"
his love of life's "dark allurement," but not his determinism; or
Anderson's "more thorough imaginative equipment," which
ranks his stories among the best of American life; or Mary
Vorse's *Growing Up* for its "true realism . . . with good old-
fashioned story-telling." He rates Frank Swinnerton as "the
finest artist now writing in English fiction!" He praises Beres-
ford, Shaw, Maugham, Wells; he rejects Cabell's *Beyond Life*
and writes that soon literature will break out in "Bolshevik fu-
ry" and sweep away the "little 'movements' and 'modernities'"

which are "no more than symptoms of the decay of the great literary traditions of the past."

In 1919 he notes a "new kind of fiction—the Novel of Proletarian Revolt, which seems to me the destiny in which the political novel will find its fulfillment." He defines such a novel as one which "gives us the psychology of a class rather than of individuals—least of all, of individuals in the familiar situation of romantic love." He praises Russia for a new art program that submits the work to a jury of the people; and, glossing over the straitjacket effect of "democracy of the herd," he declares: "Tolstoi was right after all: art must be *of and for and by the people!*" He interprets this statement to mean that art is "to share deep emotions with others." Later, after declaring himself for communism, he argues that in Russia the concern now is with reconstruction, not revolution, and that a novelist can look back and deal with "old hopes and dreams of the revolutionary cause," but that, since America is still in the "pamphlet and soapbox stage," such "revolutionary" impulses must stabilize before he will write about them himself.

In saying that "fiction at its best deals with actions, and with ideas only as illustrated in action," he defines what is his own method of evoking the "past in terms of experience and emotion. . . ." As novelist he will keep politics and art clearly separate. His review of Helen Martin's story of Pennsylvania Dutch home life and family problems anticipates his own concerns as novelist: what goes on inside "the Home is still, in spite of Ibsen and Shaw, a Dark Continent whose dank and terrifying jungles will require exploration for another fifty years at least before the gruesome secrets are discovered."

Just as politics and the novel were for Dell separate provinces, so poetry was a kind of private experience of self and dreams that became an "utter transport from the world of reality into a realm of imagination." Poetry involved pain and pleasure, and, by 1919, in a review of Eastman's poetry, Dell was asking for the "glad poem" of a Sappho or Pindar, for poems with the "pleasure-motif," hope, "yea-saying." Old favorites are reaffirmed: the psychological curiosity of Browning, the pioneering of Whitman, the primeval elements in Sandburg; he rejects Masters for his pre-Darwinian psychology and Pound for his retreat "built out of fragments from the Ming Dynasty and the Yellow Book." Tanselle has called the dualism of "art and socialism" the most "pervasive feature" of Dell's writings, and he notes that this duality became more apparent in *The Liberator* work than in earlier radical magazines.[42] Dell has acknowledged the conflict himself; it is one that will appear over and over in the novels.

Then in October, 1918, Dell met B. Marie Gage, who had just moved to the Village from California. Born in Minnesota, "golden-haired and blue-eyed," Miss Gage had gone to the University of Wisconsin, was an active Socialist, and had once been fined under the Espionage Act for selling a pacifist book. She and Dell had much in common, and he fell in love with her at once. Friends gave the marriage six months. "I knew it was forever," he writes; and he was right. They were married February 8, 1919; and, in April, they bought a house in Croton-on-Hudson, where the Mount Airy Group—some called it a suburb of Washington Square—included John Reed, Stuart Chase, Boardman Robinson, and Max Eastman. In what Dell has called a year of "great hopes and terrible disillusionments," he was happily at work. After a walking trip in New England, he wrote "Literature and the Machine Age"; and that autumn he revised *The Liberator* essays on education and published them as *Were You Ever a Child?*

VI   Were You Ever a Child?

In his review of *Were You Ever a Child?,* Max Eastman wrote that ". . . there is hardly a better educated man in the United States than Floyd Dell." The praise is ironic, for Dell's education had come mostly from his own reading and experience. With a point of view that is partly social revolutionary and partly good sense, and working in the progressive tradition of John Dewey and Randolph Bourne, Dell had written a kind of educational autobiography that tells much about his own problems as a child and as a young artist coming to terms with the "real world." Using the question-answer technique of organization and an easy, casual language that makes complex material seem easy, Dell explains the "ideals and methods" of experimental schools that were, he felt, providing the educational directions of the future. *Were You Ever a Child?* is partly Dell's own "intellectual pilgrimage" as well as a treatise on education.

Dell defines education as "an adjustment between the child and the age in which he lives" (viii). A proper education, he believes, should enable the child to "feel that he is a useful and important part of our world" (23) and to discover "what the world of reality is like" (25). Discovery means the chance "to observe, touch, handle, take apart and put back together again, play with, work with, and become master" of that "real world outside" (26). Real learning begins when the natural curiosity of the child questions something; and teachers, acting not as "Immaculate Omniscience" but as friendly guides, show and tell. Books are helpful—and here Dell might be following Emerson—but they are not "Omniscience Itself."

As Dell sees our educational system, it is based on sex and class. Men are educated one way; women, another. Often an education is a matter of status; and, although some are finally educated, others do not attend school or can not; and many are bored. Although the trade unions in the 1830's had opposed purely technical education and, joined by popular response, had succeeded in maintaining "book-learning" for all, schools later had been dominated by the spirit of Prussian uniformity and had been so systemized and regulated that, as a result, education faltered. If man is to be his own master, and not a slave, he must remain the forever questioning "child" who has not forgotten "how to play," how to embody "one's own creative wishes, one's own dreams" (91).

Expressed in eighteenth-century abstractions, the aim of education is, as Dell writes, to achieve beauty, truth, and goodness; but he redefines these terms as "the cultivation of the creative faculties, of disinterested curiosity, and of personal relationships . . ." (98). But the child is naturally endowed; no one teaches him to create beauty. He is born an artist, already creating. Beauty cannot be argued about; "it can only be produced," for it is the "incidental result of the effort to create a house, a sword," or "a shoe" (103). And while art and consequently beauty have their origin and destiny in "the production of useful things," other impulses are involved in the process of creating: the impulse to impose one's will on the material; the respect one has for what the material *"wants done* to it" (106). What Dell calls the vanity and reverence in man, "when . . . set free in the dream and effort of creation, produce something which is more than useful. That *something more* is what we call Beauty" (107). "Truth," writes Dell, "is reality brought into vital contact with the mind" (153). It is in this "contact of the child through the medium of curiosity" and perhaps in moments of idleness that "reality" is perceived. Likewise, goodness is a matter of "civilized relationships between persons," especially in the areas of work and love (158). People "prefer to work," Dell believes; they like "difficulties for their own sake"; but they judge an act in terms of how it relates to a world of reality or of fantasy that they can understand. Goodness involves reaching out: it is realization that the creativity of something useful or desirable to others adds another quality, and that the creating demands the child's—or the man's—responsibility of doing what he commits himself to do as a free human being.

As an educational treatise that describes Dell's own "intellectual pilgrimage," *Were You Ever a Child?* is also a kind of prologue to the novels. In working out his concept of "a social ideal which includes sexual and family responsibility" and in the chapters on the child and artist and the "real world"—nearly half of the book—Dell writes about the problems of growing up, of becoming an artist, of love and marriage, and of the necessity for personal adjustment to the real world—problems that concern him in writing fiction. As he says: ". . . art springs from the commonest impulses of the human race, and those impulses are utilitarian at root. . . . When art becomes divorced from the aspirations of the common man, all its technical perfection will not keep it alive . . ." (122). Out of man's contact with reality come beauty, truth, goodness. The task of education, like the task of the novel, is "to make realities more interesting than dreams"; and that task will demand our "Enterprise, and Democracy, and Responsibility," our work and our love.

CHAPTER 4

The Felix Fay Trilogy

IN A SENSE, Dell's publication of a novel had been a long time coming. To be certain, he had written and published short stories in Davenport, Chicago, in Greenwich Village; but the story that was to become the first two novels and finally the Felix Fay trilogy was not to take shape until after World War I. At the end of the war and with the resolution of many personal problems, he had "begun again to be an author" with his volume on education and his long essay on literature and the machine age; but chapters of the novel remained in a formative stage. Still working on the *Liberator* staff, he began suddenly to have blinding headaches. There was a slight sinus condition, but he knew "the cause might be psychic." As he says, "I was homesick for work on my novel, and unwilling to postpone it." He took a leave of absence in February, 1920, from duties on *The Liberator* and set to work on the novel.

Already the 1920's had settled into a mold of prosperity and disillusionment; but, as Merle Curti has observed, many of the attitudes of revolt commonly ascribed to the 1920's had appeared before the war: "the movement for greater opportunities for women, the self-consciousness of youth, the waxing prohibition crusade, the revolt against middle-class respectability and the genteel tradition, the activities of the underworld—none of these was new."[1] After the war, amid disarmament talks and peace pacts, a return to "normalcy" had brought deep disillusionment and a righteous pacifism. Although some like Dell and Eastman had continued to support Russia, popular reaction against international idealism and any form of socialism or communism increased during the decade. America retreated from any thought of foreign entanglement, whether "industrial, intellectual, or political," to glory in its own superiority. An emphasis on "Nordic" strains gave support to the Ku Klux Klan. The writing of social protest and revolutionary reform began to fade; but in 1920, "by an astonishing coincidence," a number of writers, both old and new, many of them from the Middle West, came forth with sharply drawn observations and comments about American life. One of the new novelists was Floyd Dell.

Actually, Dell had been writing novels for a long time—ever since the Davenport days. But his unsuccessful attempts had taught him that "a novel deals with the lives of people as they extend in the dimension of time"; that changes "are foretold, predicted, by small but significant events"; and that he had "never known anybody long enough to see much happening to them in the way of change," unless, of course, it was himself.[2] He also found the Norris, London, Sinclair school of propaganda too limiting; "only Ibsen," as far as he knew, "had achieved both truth of social situation and truth of individual character. . . ." When he found both qualities in Robert Herrick's *Together,* he was inspired. "From that time forward," he recalls, "the novel became more interesting to me, less miraculously a matter of dazzling verbal gifts and more a matter of telling observed and experienced truths, a matter more in my line."[3]

But many years passed before he completed a novel; and then, as he recalls, the story about Felix Fay "originated in my reading of Tolstoi's 'Childhood, Boyhood and Youth,' and was given a certain form as a result of talking with [Arnold] Bennett."[4] He began to set down what he could remember of his own childhood. "I tried to trace some sort of development in my mind from the child I glimpsed in the past on down to me in the present. . . ."[5]

When Dell talked with Bennett in Chicago, the novelist told him "that it was growing up in a small town that gave one the knowledge of people necessary for novel writing. A novelist, he said, learns everything he knows about people before—I think he said twenty-one years of age, possibly earlier."[6] Reflecting on the fact that he had grown up in not one small town but three, Dell resolved to "write the story of a youth whose character was formed by his having been uprooted from one environment after another; such a youth would not be a settled and regular person—he would be me."[7] After coming to New York, he had made progress: he had named the hero Felix Fay, thought of the title *Moon-Calf,* and outlined the first chapters. Psychoanalysis had helped him "to select the emotionally important incidents and people in my youthful life, and to emphasize certain aspects of these."[8] But the writing was slow and sometimes painful. As he has recalled, he actually disapproved of Felix's character and behavior.

By 1920 the nearly thirty thousand words Dell had written had been revised and polished into a "prose poem"; but he was not satisfied. Beginning again, he rewrote the story in three months, using "a simpler and more flexible and narrative style"; and he played down the hero's energies, making him into a "shy, lonely sensitive youth," the sentimental dreamer Felix Fay.

Building Felix's character from his own experience in growing up, Dell avoided the "tricks of style" he detested. To him, writing stories "consists very simply in the imaginative dramatization of the idea. One must know the characters—they must be oneself or/and those one loves or hates or has thought about a great deal."[9] Working within the traditional framework of the autobiographical novel, Dell traces the development of a rebellious and sensitive boy at the turn of the twentieth century. Yet the narrative of Felix Fay is not mere autobiography but the story of Dell's alter ego; and, just as Dell had reflected and partly shaped the ideas and attitudes of his generation, so Felix Fay is likewise both an individual and a type. As Orrick Johns has asserted: "Floyd Dell, in Mooncalf [*sic*], had written about the life of all of us."[10]

I Moon-Calf

Although *Moon-Calf* was sometimes construed as an "exposé of the Middle West," it is, as Dell writes in the dedication, the "record" of that region's "grim yet generous hospitality to the fantastic beauty of young American life." Young Felix's revolt derives not from his hatred and contempt for his small-town environment but from his realization that he cannot remain there and be free. Like *The Briary-Bush* and *Souvenir, Moon-Calf* is the story of youth on a journey of exploration and discovery, of youth seeking the mystery of growth and of self, and of achievement and success. Just as the characters are "pilgrims on an unknown pilgrimage," so the controlling stylistic pattern of *Moon-Calf, The Briary-Bush* and, to a lesser extent, of *Souvenir,* as well as many subsequent novels, is the pilgrimage, the quest of a moon-struck boy.

In shaping his material, Dell seems fully aware that physical wandering reflects the inner restlessness, the questioning growth, the developing sensibility of his hero. He recalled later that "the scene broadened, chapter by chapter, from the home to the yard and then to the school and the outside world, as the boy grew older; the passage of the years was stated partly in terms of expanding geography."[11] The geographical pattern of *The Briary-Bush* is one of Chicago streets; that of *Moon-Calf,* one of towns. Felix's inner growth is the movement from the village of Maple (the Barry, Illinois, of Dell's youth) to the town of Vickley (Quincy, Illinois), and to the city of Port Royal (Davenport, Iowa). *Moon-Calf* is the story of a sensitive lad who tries to cultivate his creative faculties, his disinterested curiosity, his personal relationships and his childlike wonder in a stultifying adult world. His ultimate aim is a kind of ideal happiness; and, since the name Felix Fay means happiness and sprite, his real search is for the meaning of his own identity.

Using a technique that he employed in subsequent novels, Dell begins *Moon-Calf* with a brief narrative history of the hero's family; but he focuses on the elements of revolt and idealism that have characterized it. Grandfather Fay is an Abolitionist and farmer, whose youngest son has broken away from the iron tyranny of his father's domination and enlisted in the army. Wounded and later imprisoned, the son returns after the war to the butcher shop in Maple, still rebellious and determined in his ways. He marries a schoolteacher; rears a family, including the frail young Felix; votes the Republican ticket; and dreams of a prosperous life that never materializes. Life for the Fays, a lonely existence in a thinly cultured region, is beset by economic and social poverty.

Although related to the context of his family, the story of young Felix's own pilgrimage lies in his growing awareness of the realities of life about him. An important step in his pilgrimage of self-understanding is the lesson in egotism. As a sensitive child, lost in a world of egocentric ideas and ideals, Felix finds the "outside world" strange, cruel, and bewildering. He lives in a "world of dreams," a "land of shapes," which form reality for him. His first remembered act is one of revolt: when his sister is shut in the garret for punishment, Felix defies "the mysterious and terrible order of his universe" and knocks the brace from the door. Going to school leads to a widening world; the discovery of sex, mostly in a "doctor book" in the attic, takes him into "a part of the mysterious and troublesome real world which he feared and disliked" (64). In showing how events impinge on the boy's consciousness and how the boy in turn reacts to them, Dell portrays Felix's inner growth through the boy's memories and desires.

In moving to Vickley, Felix becomes slowly aware of his relationship to an economic world that nearly defeats his family. Recognition for his ability to speak and write wins Felix a place for himself at school. After reading Robert Ingersoll and Ernst Haeckel, he questions the past and ceases to believe in God and the Republican party; he learns to curse "institutions, the traditions, the restrictions, the cruelty and the waste of Christian civilization" (118). Working in a candy factory fosters his own self-sufficiency; discovering socialism aggravates his rebellion against economic injustice and increases his loathing for the poverty and economic insecurity of his own family and his own life.

In Port Royal, the most important of the three towns, Felix begins to evaluate his past: he sees that in Vickley he "had been part of the human process," had known "the feeling of communion with the race." Now, "flung out into an utterly alien world," he has again lost his "old self-sufficiency." Lonely, he turns to poetry; and Dell's analysis describes the thought patterns of the boy's mind:

Through streets that were not the streets he knew by day, down light-and-shadow-enchanted ways, Felix wandered by night, making his songs. He knew now that he was a poet. . . .

He had found happiness at last. It seemed that he entered, at first only for moments, and then for long golden hours, an enchanted land in which there was neither desire nor fear—only the solace of magic words.

He grew indifferent to the outer world. It seemed less real to him than this realm of dreams into which he was able to transport himself in an instant. (163)

But the dream is only escape; "he must live in the world of reality" (165).

Although, like Dell, Felix drops out of school, his education continues—as Dell advocated in *Were You Ever a Child?*—through the processes of actual living. The town librarian (Marilla Freeman in real life) makes him aware of his clumsy social abilities but praises his conversational brilliancy and introduces him to literary people. Tom Alden (based on George Cram Cook) calls him a "sprite," a "fay," and talks books and ideas with him. Working once more in a candy factory where he learns "in a blundering and painful way . . . the uses of the real world" (199), Felix is tolerated and liked as a human being; he is "in this scene but not of it." But socialism, which supplies both an understanding and a refuge, is like "coming home" "after a long exile" (212). What appeals to Felix is what had appealed to Dell: the intellectual stimulation that new ideas and attitudes can give.

Felix's education by the Socialists comes partly from Comrade Vogelsang, mail-carrier and critic (Fred Feuchter in real life), who reads the boy's poetry; he tells Felix: "You have been mooning about, writing verses about life, instead of living. You have been afraid to live. Most people are. Something stands between them and life. Not only economic conditions: something else—a shadow, a fear" (218). This man's thoughts, derived from an alien culture, have "dazed as well as illuminated" young Felix. In assessing the boy's writing, Vogelsang tells him: "You are the victim of what you have read. I do not say you copy what others have written. I only say that you have discovered in yourself only what other poets have revealed to you in yourself" (221). He urges Felix to read Dostoevsky, Ibsen, and Shaw in order to unlearn the accumulations and "debris of stale culture."

Socialist theory also supplies both descriptive and prescriptive truths that help Felix understand the world of economics that he has already encountered. He sees that he has been made to work beyond his physical capacity in the candy factory and that his dismissal from his job after the Christmas rush are but instances of capitalist exploitation. He learns a lesson in practical politics: even at a Socialist meeting democratic methods may elect fools and connivers. He begins to gain a "profound self-confidence" and enough self-knowledge to choose "what he *wanted* to do."

In becoming a newspaper reporter, Felix believes that his new position will enable him to meet all kinds of people, "to experiment with life, to learn what he himself was really like . . ." (259). After two years, he has become dramatic critic on the newspaper; he lives in a "small and ordered world"; his ego feeds on a "succession of small triumphs." He has been happy in his little flirtation with Mrs. Miller, in listening to Rabbi Nathan's sermons (Rabbi Fineshriber in real life), in attending Socialist meetings, and in founding the Monist society with Tom Alden. But other lessons are still to be learned.

Felix's education in Book Four is largely a matter of moral growth that revolves around love and sex. The episode with Joyce Tennant not only jolts him into new awareness but enables Dell to present one of his "modern" women and to show Felix as a developing thinker with what were—and still may be—advanced and shocking ideas. Joyce Tennant is radically different. Without close family ties, like so many of Dell's characters, she smokes and makes love. She has been expelled from college for breaking nearly every rule. She believes in freedom of action and decision; she has more interest in short-term affairs than in long-term principles. A rather ordinary person, she seeks ordinary happiness. Felix tries to explain his beliefs in socialism, in God, and in love without owning each other; but he never really convinces her of his ideas or wins her. She marries another; and Felix, having lost his job on the newspaper, decides to go to Chicago.

Although by the end of the story the moon-calf idealist has been shaped into an innocently serious intellectual with enough maturity and sophistication to provide a certain objectivity in his point of view, he is still in the formative stage, still more devoted to abstractions than to real life. Even if he is on the outside of things, he is not an alien; he is neither disillusioned nor angry. More than anything else, whatever wisdom he has somehow achieved, he is still impelled by the personal idealism of the poor boy seeking success.

Published in October, two days after Lewis' *Main Street, Moon-Calf* was, after some delay, well received. In November, Heywood Broun advised readers: "Drop whatever you are doing and read Floyd Dell's Moon-Calf. . . ." Arturo Giovannitti, writing in *The Liberator,* asserted that Felix was more than "an American type"; ". . . he is to be found always and everywhere in every age and clime." Robert Benchley, noting that Felix "is not an ordinary boy by any means," declared that he is "not a successful anything." Kenneth Burke said that Dell's words "develop a dull and unpenetrative edge while his form is not at all illuminative." Although reviewers constantly compared the novel with Zona Gale's *Miss Lulu Bett* and with Sherwood Anderson's *Poor White,* Dell said that Lewis' work, *Main Street,* helped carry his own novel along "to a considerable sale." By January, 1922, *Moon-Calf* had had eleven printings.

For awhile, Dell and Lewis engaged in public comment on their work, But Dell's comment on *Main Street* tells more about himself than about Lewis' novel. Dell deplored the fact that Lewis' idealistic heroine had submitted to "forces of convention and commercialism," "not merely because the town is dull, but because she is weak." He saw no reason why the idealist need be either a "victim of commercialism or an exile from it." Even if there is "something essentially silly about all young idealism," it remains "one of the most beautiful things in the world."[12] Lewis, less critical, believed that Dell's economics and his "graceful genius for loafing, and for smiling at pretty, adorable things" had made *Moon-Calf* remarkable, a book "unchanneled by magazines." He thought of Dell as discussing the Third International but as wishing all the while that he were on the Isle of Aengies "where they sleep and sing and make verses and make love and haven't yet heard about even the First International." Dell, he said, was but "a faun at the barricades!"[13]

As Ima Herron has rightly pointed out, Dell "championed disturbed youth against restricting social tyrannies"; he added "to the small town of modern fiction a new type of citizen— the youthful dreamer, or seeker of a mad ideal, who feels . . . that a small town environment is antagonistic to his cultural de-

velopment."[14] Although *Moon-Calf* portrays an individual's rebellion, Dell had no intention of writing a "radical" novel of
"strikes, lynchings and working-class misery." He had written it
to please himself; he had tried to tell the truth about his hero
and about his relationship to the world in which he lived. If the
Emersonian idea of a person's doing his own "thing" were sensational—and it was and still is—Dell's use of language was neither shocking nor experimental. Felix Fay comes to life as a
character precisely because he is warmly real and human in his
dreams and fears and because he is diminished in the heroic
sense to be like all those who are sensitive and weak and wish to
succeed. The live element of the novel lies partly in the idea of
the growth of the moon-struck boy and partly in the amusingly
whimsical and gracefully informal writing that is meticulously
simple, although the material is deceptively complex. With Felix
Fay, Harry Hansen said, came "the beginnings of the American
intellectual radical who refuses to accept what comes down to
him from other ages and other times, but only that which his
own judgment tells him is good."[15]

II The Briary-Bush

Originally, Dell had planned to end *Moon-Calf* "with the
dreamer's purposeful adaptation of himself to reality in marriage"; but, as the novel grew, he changed his plan and ended it
with Felix's decision to go to Chicago. *The Briary-Bush* (1921),
therefore, simply completes Dell's original plan: the hero's
youthful dream of success, still impelled by the poor boy's personal idealism, takes literal shape as Felix succeeds in love and
marriage and in the literary and intellectual worlds. In planning
The Briary-Bush (the title comes from an old song about marriage), Dell uses a series of streets as the informing pattern of
the novel. As the hero and heroine pursue their separate and
finally mutual quest of self-fulfillment, streets become focal
points for their intellectual, artistic, and emotional developments.

For Felix—and surely for Dell—Chicago is a symbol of newfound freedom and of the "real world"—the culmination in size
and complexity of all the towns Felix has thus far known; and

to go there is to stop being "Felix Fay the fool, the poet, the theorist" (4) and to become a "young man of action"; to test his ability in confronting the hard facts of life; to discover life's meanness, if any, and come to grips with it. Having burned his novel about Port Royal, Felix faces Chicago as if he were a beginner, armed only with a "paper sword" of introduction. Once in the city, he finds that "the points of the compass seemed . . . to have got strangely twisted" (28); but, in his geographical meandering, he not only gains further insights into his expanding world and growing sensibilities but achieves personal and public success. With a background that unites staunch individualism and social purpose, Felix dreams of reform; but the dream that he is "destined to help bring back to English fiction its lost candour, the candour of the Elizabethans and Defoe and Fielding" (19) has more literary connotation than economic; and it suggests that Dell's major relation to his age is that of artist. To a "moon-calf" idealist, Chicago is neither escape nor retreat; it is a unique and genuine experience, although at times a very painful one.

Felix begins the journey that allows him to "be a fool and dreamer and yet make terms with Chicago" at the Community House, a kind of comfort station on his pilgrimage that makes the transition from Port Royal to Chicago a rather easy matter. Actually, this "gathering place for idealists of all sorts and kinds" (35) is not unlike a small town or village itself. In the assorted types that he finds there, Felix sees a bit of himself in the young man from Arkansas with the British accent and a love for stage art and *The Yellow Book,* or in the fellow from Nevada who affected evening clothes and worshiped Baudelaire. As Dell himself knows and as Clive Bangs seems to demonstrate: a man can write editorials for a conservative newspaper and still remain "inwardly an Anarchist, a Utopian, a theorist and dreamer of the wildest sort. . ." (54). Felix teaches a class in writing at the settlement house, meets Rose-Ann Prentiss, who shows him that "Bab Ballads," and not a street-map, is the better guide to Chicago and that success is built not on the cultivation of a manner or cliché but on insight and imagination evolved from personal effort. He falls in love with her; finds himself a job as a journalist; and, during her absence in Springfield, he leaves the protection of communal living and finds a place of his own on Canal Street, an address that suggests the assertion of his old rebellious spirit, his need for independence and freedom.

The gang of crazy Bohemians he runs into demonstrates how easily good intentions go astray, especially for a dreamer in love. Felix at first regards his Canal Street room as "being a quiet backwater, out of reach of the tides of life" (94), where he proposes "to write—what, he did not know yet: and it did not matter: something, anything, a play, a poem, a story—whatever came into his head, good or bad" (89). The truth is that he is avoiding both life and his own emotions, although he moves in a wild world of Bohemian living, rife with cigarettes, whiskey, and coffee; with talk of Swinburne and Flaubert; with much philosophizing *about* life. Such a life leads to neither writing nor fame; for Felix it ends, rather, with pneumonia, the hospital, and a period of convalescence at Clive Bangs's place in Woods Point. During this period he and Rose-Ann, who returns to Chicago after the death of her mother, decide to marry.

The Briary-Bush is more than the story of Felix Fay and his private search for success as a writer; the central problem of the novel, as the title suggests, is that of the love and marriage of two young idealists who are seeking independence and freedom. As unconventional in her views as Felix, Rose-Ann belongs to a list of heroines that Dell has created from his already articulated ideas and ideals for the freedom of women in both work and play. Originally a prude, Rose-Ann has been converted to paganism on reading Whitman's *Leaves of Grass.* Looking at her body in the mirror, she wants to be a dancer; but she realizes that, to be one, she should have begun as a child. She has come to Chicago to do settlement work, although she is still too troubled to be fully aware of her own mind. She assures Felix that her idea of marriage is not one of just home, children, security; instead, she wants freedom for herself "to go on living my own life outside the home" (107) and freedom for each of them. If she were brave enough, she would dispense altogether with the marriage ceremony.

The storm center that their marriage becomes is a tangle of contradiction between the personality of each and with each other; between a conventional heritage, which they can not

quite overcome, and unconventional ideas, which they have ac-
quired; between artistic temperament, which they cultivate, and
bourgeois desires, which they try to suppress. And, while their
problems remain personal, the drama of their private lives, enacted before a limited group but in the public arena, becomes
part of the intellectual and artistic excitement of the city.

Especially the sections entitled "Fifty-seventh Street" and
"Garfield Boulevard," although there are many other episodes
throughout the novel, are literary history. Using himself and his
own marriage to Margery Currey as a basis for much of the narrative, Dell can hardly be expected to see his Chicago years in
other than personal terms. What has become a significant chapter in the literary history of America necessarily remains for
him a private history of the fulfillment of personal needs and
desires. In another sense, perhaps in the real sense, a historical
episode may be only personal events and decisions publicized, so
that, in trying to convey the nature of real life as he saw and
knew it, he has provided as accurate a history of the "Chicago
renaissance" as we have had.

In life, the Dell and Currey studios on Fifty-seventh Street
and Stony Island Avenue had become centers for artists and intellectuals; and, while Dell alters the facts to fit the imaginative
construct of his story, the studio-salon on Fifty-seventh Street
to which Felix and Rose-Ann move after their marriage becomes
a symbol of protest against traditional and conventional re-
straints, as well as an intellectual haven for all those who long
for moral and intellectual freedom. The studio serves as the geographical high point for many a "bewildered wanderer" in
search of liberation.

Living in the studio is as much evasion of Felix and Rose-
Ann's problems as solution. There is uncertain freedom in living
without table cloths, "sets of dishes," bathroom facilities, and
central heating. There is questionable joy in reducing life to the
barest essentials: two work tables, two beds, "ordinary kitchen
chairs," books and dishes. Although this return to minimum essentials spells out as with Thoreau their protest against conventions and tradition, the problems of adjusting to each other and
to life itself remain. The series of parties that they give for their
intellectual and artistic friends only help to avoid the real issues

of their demands for individual joy and freedom. As Dell makes clear, success in marriage, like artistic success, demands that people cope with their dreams and illusions: real life, both for the people living it and for the artist portraying it, is not the same as the dreamer's dream of it.

Actually, for Felix, success as artist and success in marriage are related. Although he has gained fame as a dramatic critic, he has not succeeded as a playwright. Still curious and observant, he is also evasive and indecisive. Dell's use of an oil portrait of Felix that a friend has done is both autobiographical and good technique: just as Dell in real life had been painted in all his suave arrogance, so Felix sees himself and realizes that being an artist demands "calm energy, . . . technical erudition, . . . vast patience" (259). Although by living apart in a separate room, he feels free enough to create and does produce a play, he has also forgotten "Rose-Ann, his marriage, his home, his plans, his future" (319); and he has fallen in love first with Phyllis Nelson, who is engaged to his friend Clive Bangs, and later with Elva Macklin, who performs a part in his play. In following his impulses, he has become a vagabond and a fool.

Comprehending self and coping with the real world come slowly to Felix. As the "foundations" of his "existence seemed to crack and fall apart," so the "whole edifice of thought and emotion in which he lived" toppled and tumbled "in ruins" (317). Felix knows that he has "to adjust this thing that had happened, to all the rest of his life, to Rose-Ann, to his marriage, to his career" (319). At first, he is overcome by "some mysterious inward paralysis"; but, when Rose-Ann leaves for a magazine assignment in California and he moves to Wilson Avenue, he then feels "that a new life had begun for him, a life at which he still stared in vague bewilderment, like a creature painfully new-born into an uncomprehended world" (355). Actually, he does not yet fully comprehend; he is still primarily the dreamer.

The happy outcome of Felix and Rose-Ann's marriage in *The Briary-Bush* is fictional representation, not of the failure of Dell's first marriage but of the success of the second. As he says in *Homecoming* of the novel's ending, "it was what one wishes one's life had been like."[16] Perhaps separation, time, and travel have somehow redressed the balance between revolt and respectability. Only partly consoled by the song about the briary-bush of marriage that Elva Macklin sings to him, and partly amused at the foolish things they do, he feels like an outsider and stranger to all his old dreams and illusions. The psychic distance helps him to write, not only of people "as they were," but also "of himself as he had been—caught hopelessly in the briary-bush of human passions" (381). He now sees that, while emotions and ideas are a profound mystery, some incidents between two individuals are only a quarrel. Quarrels can be righted. Indeed, quarrels are part, whether essential or not, of the human pattern.

Felix and Rose-Ann are reunited in California, where they finally realize that they have both been afraid of life and its beauty. They have also been misled by a dream of freedom that was "worthy only the farewell tribute of a faint and shadowy regret" (425). If the successful artist succeeds by practicing mostly what are old-fashioned virtues, so success in marriage demands an emotional maturity that can redefine freedom, not as the bent of one's will or even as an ideal, but as the relationship between individuals whose honesty and integrity spring from a knowledge of real life. Indeed, both revolt and respectability are part of that life; and, when Felix and Rose-Ann think in terms, not of a studio, but a house, they move toward the conventional; if they have but played at marriage and been afraid of life, the house they plan to build has more respectability about it than iconoclasm. Yet the knowledge, the curiosity, the freedom for which they have always stood remain integral to their moral, intellectual, and esthetic goal.

With the two volumes on Felix Fay, Dell had clearly established himself as a novelist. Contemporary opinion ranked him with Lewis, Fitzgerald, and Anderson. His was a new voice which defended the young and championed their rebellion and desire for personal freedom. Reviewers gave less praise to *The Briary-Bush* than they had to *Moon-Calf*; Heywood Broun, who had thought "that the first story of Felix Fay is one of the permanently fine novels of our period," found *The Briary-Bush* "not completely satisfactory . . . because it is a novel about a newspaper man with the newspaper all but left out." Essentially rejecting the novel, Francis Hackett praised Dell as "clearly master of his quiet, slow, mild mood as a narrator." Mary Colum thought that "the fluffy idealism of Felix Fay and the hardly-disciplined thinking" of the book make it "a very feeble performance." Although such judgments now have mostly a historical interest, they gave the novels a needed publicity.

Half a century later Dell's story of Felix may seem old-fashioned and less shocking than it did in the 1920's, but the portrait of the young idealist who seeks to follow his own inclinations is neither fluffy idealism nor the work of undisciplined thought. Dell's concept of an intellectual and sensitive youth wandering from one geographical point to another and of the corresponding growth within attests his ability to shape a novel with both structure and insight.

Although Dell's use of language is neither experimental nor deliberately symbolic, his diction is simple, clear, and precise. An example from *Moon-Calf,* in which Dell is telling about the formation of the Monist Society in Port Royal, suffices to indicate the style:

> Early the next morning, as Felix was just about to leave the office, a man came in and asked for him. He was a small, stoop-shouldered man, whom Felix had seen somewhere before. He introduced himself as Wilfred Endicott. He wanted to see "Mr. Fay" in regard to a new free-thought society which was just being formed. (283)

The tone is even, the movement slow, and the pace of the prose suggests the slow growth of the hero's character. From such mild-mannered narration emerge the thoughts and feelings of the characters as they cope with the problems and events of their little lives.

Dell's use of point of view is both personal and elusive: actually, he gently mocks his hero with ironic affection. As in the passage above, the writing has an easy humor; there is an occasional pun as, for example, the "Monist" becomes the "Moonist Society." Dell's prose seems permeated with the smile of the indulgent author who knows that life is often both foolish and successful. What makes Felix so "young" is the high seriousness and righteous conviction with which this very young man pursues his "ideal." Felix Fay is both tedious and amusing.

Although Felix's story has autobiographical significance, Dell was particularly careful to distinguish between fact and fiction.

What he says about his own aims and methods in creating
character is applicable to the writing of all fiction:

> . . . It is a mistake to suppose . . . that in writing "Moon-Calf" and "Briary-
> Bush" I was simply recounting the facts of my own life. I actually left out
> many things that happened, and changed various incidents for fictional
> purposes. . . . In the book on the Chicago Renaissance there is something
> about a play I wrote for the Hull House players. This refers to something
> in "Briary-Bush" which I invented. I had decided to make Felix a play-
> wright, not a novelist, and I put in various bits as suitable to that career.
> The fact is that in both "Moon-Calf" and "Briary-Bush" I had, to begin
> with, an *idea* about my character, a conception of him, as a fictioneer has
> of any and all characters, and I put in incidents, remembered or invented
> or altered, to substantiate that character. Well, some critics who are them-
> selves incapable of inventing a story have supposed that I never invented
> my stories but only reported what had happened to me; they sometimes
> praised me for my fidelity to facts—without knowing (how could they?)
> whether I was reporting fact or devising fictions. . . .[17]

In *The Briary-Bush,* to refer only to that novel, there is much of
Francis Hackett in Hawkins; of Charles Hallinan and George
Cook in the character of Clive Bangs; of Elaine Hyman in Elva
Macklin; of Brör Nordfeldt, the painter, in Dorothy Sheridan.
Although the studio on Fifty-seventh Street had truly existed,
there had been two of them in life. But the story of Felix Fay
remains, nonetheless, very much the story of Dell himself.

III   Souvenir

In *Moon-Calf* and *The Briary-Bush,* Dell had established his
reputation as a novelist with a hero who seemed to embody the
intellectual questioning of his generation, but he was to publish
five other novels, in addition to plays, essays, and reviews, before returning to the story of Felix Fay for the last time in
1929. *Souvenir* is not actually a continuation of *The Briary-
Bush*; instead, it is an ironic commentary by an older Felix Fay
on his own past and on the present generation, one in its teens
and twenties during the period of the "jazz age." Some of that
past emerges simply through memory: of the Chicago days,
which the reader likewise may recall from the earlier novels; of
his sojourn in Greenwich Village; of his second marriage and successful career as a playwright on Broadway. Sometimes frag-

ments of the past emerge through the reappearance of characters
from the earlier novels: Rose-Ann pays a brief visit as she stops
in New York on her way to Europe; the Clive Bangses now live
next door to Felix and his second wife; the old Socialist mail-
carrier from Port Royal turns up in Union Square. But the most
important "souvenir" is Prentiss Fay, Felix's son by his first
marriage, a boy of nineteen, who is himself something of a
wayfarer and pilgrim.

Like the two earlier volumes about Felix, *Souvenir* is the story
of youth; and, if this novel is clearly about youth in the
1920's, it is also about an older generation and its remembered
youth. The character of Prentiss serves, then, as "container" of
both past and present; he is symbol of the new generation, but
he is also a reflector of Felix's own past, a visible portrait of
his father's inner self.

Felix and his son have much in common. Like his father,
Prentiss makes a genuine attempt to write, if only for *Cowboy
Stories*. And like his father, he is often moody. In despair, he
has "brief and inconsequential adventures" in the Village: he
tries to help Helen Dorsey with her problems of career and love
and economics; he has trouble with his own love affair when his
fiancée, arriving suddenly from California, never learns the real
reason why Helen Dorsey's clothes are in his apartment. Like
his father, he can be a "charming vagabond," who is determined-
ly individualistic and who, despite prospects of an easy, generous, sensible use of his foster-father's money, prefers rebellion.

But, as Felix sees such rebellion, it has a hollow ring, as if it
were simply an end in itself. His own youth had been so different: he had worked because he had to. Poverty had not per-
mitted him time to play; consequently, he had never really felt
at home with the leisure class. Historical factors change, therefore, habits, values, and attitudes: not only has Prentiss started
with the leisure and beauty and security that money affords, he
has taken it all for granted. He is "one accustomed to all the
comforts of prosperity" (113), and he acts as if he possessed the
earth, even as if he had the right. He has worked hardest on his
game of tennis; and, as his father never did, he has grown "accustomed to wear white flannels on appropriate occasions"
(113). As Felix remembers "the Utopia of his early dreams," he

realizes that the same world that he has bequeathed to his son is not his dream but "the smug middle-class world which as a boy he had been right to hate and despise" (114). The boy, with "no resentments to placate, no pride to mollify," accepts his world with only a feeble protest or with vague indifference; he is satisfied with the status quo. Felix concludes that the new generation has gone soft: "the boy wasn't as hard as he had been" (179).

As Felix holds fast to his own conception of life, yet tries to understand his son, the visit to Prentiss's apartment on Milligan Place offers a glimpse into the very past he has resolved to avoid. Not only has Prentiss rented an apartment in the Village as his father once did, but the apartment itself takes Felix "inevitably back into the past"; for once he had "taken a girl to this door, said good-night, and gone home to Patchin Place around the corner" (157). The room and the streets are filled with memories, and he is struck by the similarity of past and present. Was there not a kind of identity between father and son? Were not the experiences of Felix's past but a premonition of his son's future? Why, then, did his son seem so difficult to understand?

As Felix begins to suspect, the difficulty of understanding lies with the past, with memory itself: it has given him a false view both of the present and of his own past. Felix sees that a man's accumulated experience and reflection, as well as the interpretations of others, have created phantoms that "distorted the simple shapes of things" (150). Prentiss is puzzle and complication to his father, not because of a fundamental difference between them, but because Felix has tried to understand the boy through the eyes of his own youth, his own egoistic personality.

As Dell seems to clarify more explicitly, youth has not lost its ideals: when Prentiss decides to go to Russia, he has not only set out on the same utopian quest as his father; he has, in his own way, always pursued the dream that has motivated his meandering and indecisiveness. If he has not found the answer, perhaps that is because the search has only begun. On his departure he tells his father: "I'll have to do something. But I'm not ready to decide about my future. I'm going to let that more or less take care of itself for a while" (277). In a sense, Felix has done exactly the same. If he has found his work at all, it is at his desk, writing. Here, as if installed in his function, he is "in control of destinies" (278).

Contemporary opinion was not kind to *Souvenir,* but the novel merits attention as part of the Felix Fay trilogy, for it amplifies the fictional history of the earlier novels and shows Dell's continued interest in the young. In comparing the two generations, Dell has emphasized what may be an essential trait in man: the spirit of rebellion, of wandering, which has, for generations, impelled the human spirit onward and upward. As Whitehead had written in 1925 and as Dell had been demonstrating in a series of novels, "when man ceases to wander, he will cease to ascend in the scale of being. Physical wandering is still important, but greater still is the power of man's spiritual adventures—adventures of thought, adventures of passionate feeling, adventures of aesthetic experience."[18]

With a little money now, Dell and B. Marie planned a family; added some conveniences to their home in Croton; and, during the summer of 1921, went on a trip to California to visit her family, stopping in Illinois on the way to see his own, and to help them by paying the fifteen hundred dollars to save their little farm. Once more Dell heard the stories of the Civil War from his father and saw the poverty that had been a part of his life, but he looked on his father and on the past with compassion. After visiting relatives and friends in southern California, they returned to New York by way of San Francisco, stopping off in South Dakota and Detroit to visit friends. By December, he had made a start on a new novel. In January, 1922, their first son was born; he was named Anthony after Dell's father. Although the world was changing into a world of jazz and disillusionment that was hardly his world, Dell held to his convictions and continued to "write the kind of novels I wanted to write." It was not until 1923, however, that he published his next novel, *Janet March.*

CHAPTER *5*

The Emerging Novelist

WITH THE publication of the Felix Fay story, Dell took his place along with Fitzgerald, Cather, and Anderson as one of the group of new fiction writers. Now in his mid-thirties, he was beginning, as it were, a third career; and, if many saw him as the successful writer with money and a vast estate, as the writer who had turned from a life of struggling radicalism to one of conservative leisure, Dell knew that he was neither young nor rich, nor did he believe himself a conservative. But with a rather "fine sense of humor," he could confess in 1921 that, although "I still like to think I'm shocking someone, and I still like to think I'm one of them; . . . the younger generation takes away my breath."[1] If his next novel, *Janet March* (1923), may not have shocked the new generation, it certainly did the old.

Published in October, *Janet March* was, as Dell says, "my first book of imaginative fiction, as distinguished from novels which were the imaginative interpretation of memories."[2] He had spent two years on it; and, just as his first novels had been "a psychological study, not a social satire," so *Janet March* "and all that followed would be of the same character."[3] Yet Dell had not completely forsaken his past; he is still the radical striving to get at the roots of man's social and political relationships. He said that as a citizen he would always be interested in politics; but, as an artist, while his "political hopes" stimulated creativity, he wished to detach himself from immediate political anxieties and "to renew my contacts with the ageless and timeless aspects of nature, which afford a deep refreshment to the restless mind."[4] The return to the "ageless and timeless aspects of nature" becomes a significant theme in the next three novels.

I   Janet March

Janet March is, as Dell writes, "in fictional terms the true story of the break up of the old patriarchal family institution in contemporary America."[5] It is the history of a family, of one Andrew March, who began his career in a livery stable in Minnesota, and whose descendant Janet becomes the thoroughly modern girl. The novel studies, therefore, three or four generations of a post-Civil War family that came to "stand for all that is considered soundest and best in American life" (5). But Dell has given age-old patterns of behavior a deeper meaning that conveys what he calls the "psychological" significance. *Janet March* is a kind of modern fairy tale with dragons and magic talismans, and the shape and telling of the novel are partly based on the typical fairy tale construction. Using the proverbial fairy tale beginning, Dell calls Book One "Once Upon a Time"; and, in Books Two and Three, he continues, as if saying there are "Janet Herself" and "Roger," and they (Book Four, "Janet and Roger") fall in love and live happily ever after.

The fairy tale construct has other implications as idea. At the moment Roger Leland begins to write, he defends fairy tales to Janet's mother, telling her that they contain "truths about life, that are left out of modern children's stories. Dragons and magic talismans: isn't life like that? If it isn't, it ought to be!" When Mrs. March asks him what they mean to Janet, he tells her that they mean "the mysteries of the grown-up world—things that you perhaps think she is too young to be curious about, but that she does wonder at, in some vague childish way" (261).

Janet's mother defines such mysteries as love and sex, but she agrees that "fairy-tales do give a truer idea of life than most children's stories," although the "symbols" often obscure "life as it is." In Book Three, Roger's belief that Janet can cope with sex, love, and life as it is becomes "a talisman" that heals "the madness in his heart" (433). If the dragon to be confronted is sex—after experience with others, in the person of Roger—the education for that confrontation becomes a major part of the novel; and the "Pilgrimage" (the title of Chapter XI) that Janet makes through the maze of this crazy world leads at last to him. He in turn has idealized her as "brave—and truthful," and so she will become, in spite of the things she has done—or perhaps because of them.

Speaking of the writer's reaction to disturbance and change, Warner Berthoff has observed that the "deeper the sentiment of rebellion and innovation, the greater the need for traditional

ways of expression. . . ."[6] In portraying the real in life, Dell recognizes that the age-old patterns of behavior in myth and fairy
tales are as psychologically true for the generation of the 1920's
as they were for generations of the past.

Although the social-historical background runs throughout
the novel, the brief initial history of the March family shows
that Janet's particular environment is also typical. Brought up
"in the American middle-class tradition of hard work" (73), old
Andrew March has lived a life of all business and no play. Out
of the thirty cents he had saved from working in a livery stable,
he has built a fortune in grain; he is honored and respected for
his harsh integrity and hard work. He knows that people drink,
play cards, dance and think ill of their home town; but he has
not been either so frivolous or so foolish, and he hopes that his
children will be as successful and practical as he. Mostly, as traditions begin to break, they are successful, if not devoted to
business, a new generation rich enough to seek a little pleasure.
With Bradford, his youngest son—Janet's father—the case is
a little different.

Although always "too much of a visionary," young Bradford
March gives up the idea of teaching literature; marries "rebel"
Penelope Rockford, whom he has met at Scott College; and returns to his father's business with more success than might have
been expected. But the ideas of Brad and Penelope differ from
those of the rest of the family: they live in a less fashionable
part of the city, give their children more freedom, remain young
in spirit, and live in an easy informal way. Their rebellion is
mild but clearly evident. If they are interested in women's rights,
in "humanizing" the "institution of family," Janet's father does
not try to change what is the "order of the world"—the "complex, and relentless machinery of modern business" (58). Rather,
the loss of a child makes him realize that "he had never become
—himself" (61); and, while he hopes that his daughter will
achieve self-realization, his uncertainty is only one of the psychological traits that, like "original sin," is visited on a new
generation.

Janet March is, as Dell says, "an attempt to present a characteristic modern girl truly against her social-historical background."[7] It is the psychological study of a young girl's growing
awareness of the world in which she lives and of her relation to

it. A tomboy, Janet grows up with a will of her own. She learns to guard her feelings against hurt and to confine to her diary her thoughts on sex and marriage, on dress and teaching, on settlement work and doing good. But she also learns to be kissed, to dance to the phonograph, to slap her escort when he is improper, to become part of the younger crowd. Part romping schoolgirl, part quasi-sophisticate, she helps, like the youth of any generation, to establish "new conventions of their own."

Her love affairs were not exactly in good taste; but, having grown up in the shadows of war and gone to college, she has learned to treat the attentions of young men with the vast indifference that convention seems to demand. As Dell writes:

A strange Puritanism ruled their behaviour; in this modern world in which they lived, a world that afforded them continual opportunities to break every code, they kept faith, after their fashion, with the social order which gave them with such confidence their freedom. The young men, when they had made a place for themselves in the world, would marry young women of whom they could trustfully assume that, notwithstanding their freedom, they had merely taken harmless boyish kisses with an air of bored indifference. Such, at least, was convention. (118)

But these seemingly safe conventions are also changing: everyone smokes and drinks; there are rumors of young men with "a horrid disease." During the war Janet spends her spare time at the Hostess House and at parties for young officers, where she acquires an attitude of "laughing scepticism about everything" (125). If the war has changed all their lives, Janet has somehow "ceased to take the laws of God and man very seriously" (125).

With a troubled mind that grows uncertain and unhappy, Janet finds it more and more difficult to make proper choices. She works as a filing clerk in an insurance company where girls "aren't wanted," "just tolerated" (154). She wonders if it is proper for anyone—not just the rich—to have lovers "in the continental sense!" (142). She falls in love with Paul Richards, whose literary interests reflect the reading of Dell and his contemporaries. And she also falls in love with Vincent Blatch, an artist and stage designer, who goes to Chicago where Janet follows him and becomes pregnant. She sees that it is a crazy world, but seeing it as such does not really explain the mysteries of her restless self.

The affair with Blatch forces her to probe deeply into the

moral nature of sex and love. Recovering from an abortion that
Blatch does not know about, Janet cannot believe that the love
of two people, no matter what the consequence, is sinful. Actually, she remembers it as beautiful, as "something antique and
noble in its very naturalness," as a "rite that took one back out
of civilization into some earlier world," as a "solemn and sacred
ceremonial of the worship of nature" (215). As Dell insists here
and elsewhere, she has learned, not what she glibly says—"this is
a crazy world"—but that love (Dell means sexual love) is an important answer to any one in "this world of bewildered wonder-
ing in the dark!" (215).

Using metaphor that is mythical, poetic, Dell writes: ". . . it
was the satisfying of some deep impersonal need, like hunger,
like thirst, like the wish for sleep; it was rest, healing, quietness
after tumult; yes, like getting back to the shady coolness of the
woods at Winga Bay after a sweltering week in the city. And it
was finding hints, through one's body, of something that might
be one's soul; it was a taking of wings and soaring into perilous
heights of ecstasy, alone" (215). And her trouble is that "her
soul had been unmated in that strange flight," and so she remains, bewildered "in the dust and darkness," although there
has been a beauty and madness, a "dazzling light, and the crash
of a gigantic wave; oblivion, and peace, . . .—kisses of gratitude"
(215).

No longer a child, she can not return to college, but goes to
New York, to Greenwich Village, and finally to Roger Leland.
As Dell has said, her journey is "a pilgrimage"; and much of the
story of *Janet March*—actually about half of the novel—belongs
to Roger Leland, whose dreams and idealism have made him an
outsider in the world of well-meaning respectability that defines
the moral code of his native Plainsburg. Having grown up with
his uncles and aunts in an implement store, he has inherited
some of his father's "love of beauty, of romance, of ease"; but
he has had difficulty in mastering the stern discipline of "work,
plan, and save" that his aunt believes will save him from such
vices as idleness and debauchery (245). Moreover, he finds but
one friend, and no one at all to love. Although books have given
him the "secrets of a larger life" (255), he wants to talk about
and make "useless and beautiful things" (256). Pursuing his

ideal with energy and egotism, he finds neither freedom nor happiness at college. Rather, he finds that the instruction in the college is "an attempt to justify the kind of life he had fled from in Plainsburg" (256).

A job in a bookstore gives him opportunity to talk about life and books, as well as to meet Mrs. Bertram March and to discuss fairy tales with her. Here he elects to remain after college, where he has earned a Phi Beta Kappa key, has been chosen class essayist, and has written stories and essays for the college monthly. But his real contact with the world comes after the death of his uncle, who leaves him a thousand dollars. As his aunt says in her letter: "Take it, and spend it on your sins, and may you rot in the gutter all the sooner" (268).

Tired of his dream life, Roger Leland begins "to look about wistfully at the real world" (269). He does not want the money, nor does he want to return it: since it has "been accumulated in a moral way," he decides it "ought to be used for some immoral purpose" (268). His venture takes him to a whorehouse, where he orders champagne, talks a great deal, and then walks out: " . . . what a dismal affair it really was—a sort of ministration to the impotency of anxious, cowardly, sick men by cold, stupid, pathetic, dull, dutiful girls. . . . They were not places of pleasure —they were hospitals for people of feeble will and diseased imagination" (285). The episode is one of the best that Dell ever wrote; he charges it with feeling and uses spare and lean language.

Although Roger aspires to the pagan and sensual in love, he discovers in his various searches that he is Puritan and Plainsburg after all—at least in part. In the long episode where he and his newfound friend Jack Squires pick up Pansy and Cecile, he seeks to test the kind of pagan love that poets have written about, not the "painful and agonized kisses of tragic love, . . . but laughing kisses, as untroubled and inconsequent as butterflies. . ." (293). But his pursuit only leaves him with a sense of "divided identity": he is a "young man who was sunk deep into the long-desired solace of this sweet and violent contact of the flesh; and the other a being aloof and disinterested, watching the scene curiously, intent upon both its actors. . ." (316). In a final gesture, he gives the rest of his money to foreign missions;

but he does not wholly return to his "old bookish habits" (341).

Dell develops the characters of Janet March and Roger Leland separately, but it becomes clear that they have comparable backgrounds; similar problems with love and sex and self; and individual searches that are necessary to their future well-being. Just as Janet's affair with Vincent Blatch has been sadly educational, so has Roger's affair with Sally Patterson. As Dell probes into the mind and motives of each and into his or her relationship to another and to the world, he involves the reader in the same search.

The affair between Roger and Sally becomes one of mutual misunderstanding that finally separates them, even before her death in Otter Lake. Having remembered her from the music store where she worked, Roger recognizes her at once in the boardinghouse where he goes to live. If he learns that this place has been her home and that she has dreamed of becoming a great singer, he does not yet understand her idealism, her pride, her faith, and her need for self-respect and love. He knows nothing of her past or of her double nature that makes her romantic and impulsive, on one hand, and "an almost sexless being," on the other.

As Dell writes, "People who live contradictory lives are given to doing things which they cannot explain, cannot tolerate in themselves, and can only, if they are to have any peace of mind, forget" (373). Indeed, both Roger and Sally are deluded by pretense: Roger thinks of her as virtuous and pretends that she should not be; she knows that she is not and pretends that she is. After their engagement ends, Roger understands that her pose was only an effort to escape from the "grotesque and ugly boarding-house world," a desire not unlike his to escape Plainsburg. Like himself, Sally had dreamed of "the upper world of leisure, of freedom, of culture, of respectability assured and complete" (394).

With Mrs. March's invitation to Winga Bay, Roger actually escapes for a little while into his "dream." As he tells Mr. March, being there is "like being out of a hateful and ugly world! It's going back to a childhood that I never had" (414). The truth is that in this "world of childhood" he meets little Janet March, who is still a child; and he speculates that, since she has grown up in a free and open life, she will believe in herself and be neither sentimental nor rebellious. "But," Roger asks Mr. March in their discussion of women and morality, "which is really to blame, a society that makes impossible rules or the girl who breaks them?" (416). In reply, March insists only that people behave sensibly and that society must learn to be tolerant. Punishment isn't the solution, for only education will help. March also insists that "human nature must learn to conform to social rules. You wouldn't . . . ask society to abandon all its rules because a few people are too impulsive to obey them?" (419).

Actually, Roger is more lost than ever, believing that he and his generation alone are "full of hatred and fears," which are complicated by lack of perspective that a past could give. But, in confronting the suicidal death of Sally, he realizes that, while she "wasn't brave enough to take life as she found it," he had done little to help her when she was alive and had threatened to kill herself. Filled with self-accusation, pity, and remorse, he finally leaves for Chicago. There on the lake-shore as he contemplates the waves, he begins to understand that life must be taken as it truly is. At least partly reconciled to events in the world, he works for awhile in a bookstore and then goes to New York.

The final chapter in which Roger and Janet are brought together is an episode of modern social history that compares with the opening chapters on old Andrew March. What was "Once Upon a Time" has become "New Times, New Manners," as if there were a new beginning in social thinking, as if the righteousness of an older generation has given way to the new "social righteousness" of broken conventions. There are still problems; for as Dell knows, simply breaking conventions is not building a new order. Roger is nearly twice as old as Janet; he is still the philosopher harboring illusions, still afraid. He can respond to her youth and even begin to write, but he is still uncertain of love, of truly loving. With their acceptance of Janet's pregnancy, they gain a feeling of certainty about each other that enables them to accept marriage just as they can now accept themselves.

Janet March is Dell's longest novel to date (over four hundred and fifty pages), but the "fairy-tale" design, the weaving of the characters' lives, the "pilgrimage" theme, and the even tone of writing give the four parts coherence. Starting at separate points and with separate family histories in what are partly separate stories, the heroine and hero eventually meet in a relationship that forms both a synthesis and a new beginning. Dell's first novel of "imagination" proves his ability at invention and attests that much of the invention was only disguised autobiography. *Janet March* contains the same ideas and themes of the earlier novels: the concern with success and idealism, with rebellion and personal freedom, with man's need to face life and see it as it is. In one sense, the novel, like all of Dell's writing, reads like an educational tract: the characters are eager for knowledge and solutions; and, whether in college like Janet March or a high-school dropout like Felix Fay, they search and wander and become pilgrims as if demonstrating that all life is learning and all learning life.

By now, Dell's characters have a set pattern of development: they rebel, they leave, they search, they find companions, they defy conventions, but finally accept them. In *Janet March* the writing is quiet and lucid; as in *Moon-Calf* and *The Briary-Bush,* the chapters are built out of a number of dramatic and narrative episodes that often makes the novel seem like a patchquilt. As each episode contributes to the unfolding of an idea that is central and, in general, very nearly the same in each novel, the reader, as if gathering the evidence, also apprehends what the character comes to understand. In *Janet March* the action is elaborated with detailed tedium; but, while the episodes on abortion, free love, suffering, and searching carry the overtones of shock, they seem to be the inevitable results of a headstrong, thoughtless idealism that has simply winked at moral values.

However shocking the novel was in 1923, Dell's interest lay more in portraying the psychology of rebellion in all men and women than in flaunting the moral bankruptcy of a new generation. Although the Felix Fay story had referred to past generations, *Janet March* ranges over a much wider social-historical landscape to explore the struggle in the minds and hearts of young men and women of several generations as they coped with their dreams and ambitions, with their bodily longings and desires, with their ideals and illusions. And Dell not only shows that each generation discovers its greed, its pride, its need for rebellion, its dreams, and its truth but that each generation discovers that it differs little from the one preceding, that cutting through the layers of pretense and meaningless respectability is always difficult, that achieving what rightfully belongs to every man and every woman is always hard: the freedom to pursue the inner longings of one's own soul, to nourish that longing with love, to exercise it "in hopes and dreams."

Although *Janet March* received mixed reviews from the press, it had, by December, 1923, become a center of controversy. Most reviewers, whether they favored it or not, saw it as a specimen of ultramodern fiction, "the true picture of the sex life of young men and women of a certain section of the middle class," as *The Bookman* said, that "transgresses the bounds of good taste. . . ."[8] Then the book was threatened with legal censorship; for, as Dell wrote at the time in a letter to a Mr. Babb in Texas and published in the Morristown, N.J., *Jerseyman* for January 26, 1924, "John S. Sumner, urged on by the Watch and Ward Society of Massachusetts, brought pressure to bear on the district attorney." In order to avoid censorship, Dell and Alfred Knopf, the publisher, agreed to suppress the novel. As a result of the conference between Knopf and New York's District Attorney Banton, Knopf withdrew the book from sale in bookstores in the states of New York and Massachusetts.

No official action was taken, therefore, against *Janet March*; and the copies in stock were allowed to be sold in bookstores outside the two states. Although Dell lost a great deal of prestige by not fighting the case, he was not eager to become involved in a lawsuit over censorship; he had been on trial twice before already. The memory of those experiences was still vivid. Advised by lawyers that "various things in the original version were liable to get me sent to prison," he revised the novel four years later—in 1927—and George Doran, his publisher at that time, issued the new version.[9] In 1924, still writing for magazines and readying the volume of essays for publication, Dell began work on a new novel, *This Mad Ideal*.

II   This Mad Ideal

This Mad Ideal, less than half the length of *Janet March*, lacks the depth of treatment that Dell had given the characters and ideas in his first three novels. While there is "modernity" in *This Mad Ideal,* there is nothing to evoke the wrath of moral censorship; the story is simply and firmly built around the social and psychological consequences of following an ideal. Although imaginative in concept, the novel, dedicated to his librarian friend in Davenport, Marilla Freeman, has many autobiographical elements in it: the rebellious nature of many of the characters, their interest in books and art and writing (one wins a prize for poetry as Dell had done), the total concern for a "mad" ideal. As he writes, Dell had aimed to make the novel "a defense" of the heroine's "choosing poetry instead of wifehood or motherhood."

The title for *This Mad Ideal* comes from Browning's poem "In a Gondola," a dramatic lyric about two lovers, in which the hero says: "Rescue me Thou, the only real!/ And scare away this mad Ideal/ That came, nor motions to depart!" As the newspaper man in the novel interprets the poem, Browning's hero has envisioned an ideal that he seeks to rid himself for "something familiar and human instead" (203). In *This Mad Ideal* Judith Valentine clings to her dream, spurns "rescue" and love, turns away from the realities of common life "to do impossible things." For Dell turning away, especially from love, was the wrong choice. As he says in *Were You Ever a Child?,* "we despise those persons who are afraid of adventure in love; who in devotion to some mawkish dream-ideal, turn away from the more difficult and poignant realities of courtship and marriage."[10]

In portraying Judith Valentine's devotion to her ideal, mawkish or not, Dell makes *This Mad Ideal* a psychological study of human conduct enacted against a background of manners and mores of a small town in New England. Beginning with the history of the heroine's family, a technique he had used in *Moon-Calf* and *Janet March,* Dell sketches a familiar pattern: the little, lonely, small-town girl finds solace in reading magazines, watching trains, and singing songs with her mother, Gloriana, who disgraces herself and family by running away to Boston and going on the stage. After a brief marriage, her career on the stage is cut short by illness and death; and Judith goes to live with her aunt and uncle in the little town of Pompton and in a world devoted to the tried and true. In Pompton, the name of Gloriana

Valentine, as Dell writes, "stood for everything that had been left out" of most people's lives, although "perhaps all of them had some misty glimmerings of a wish, an ambition, that might lead them dangerously out of the narrow paths in which they dutifully walked" (39).

Conscious of the stigma of having had a stagestruck mother who pursued her "ideal," Judith finds herself more and more of an exile in the tight little world of Pompton. Like her mother, and many another Dell character, Judith escapes not only to the "world of natural things, which offered no judgments," but "into a secret realm of imaginings" (40) where there are always new adventures in "the enchanted world of romance . . . more real to her than anything in Pompton" (72). And, like her mother, she has dreams "of life, among other people—dreams of flight, away from all this, into some place of her own" (72). Thus Judith's world of imagination and dreams is given substance through reading and books. If the old English dramatists settle no issue and give no clear view of life, they "interpret life's chaos for her" and give glimpses, along with Fielding, Defoe, and Rabelais, of other standards than those of Pompton. But her reading of Thomas Hardy leads to difficulty.

Throughout his novels, Dell shows how literature functions in the education and life of his characters; and, in the episode resulting from Judith's reading of *Jude the Obscure*, how it functions as both social criticism and plot. Caught reading the book by Principal John Quincey Sopwith, a well-meaning but "soppy" idealist, as his name suggests, Judith is bewildered by the man's diatribe against the novel and by his defense of any and all poetry that contains the "beauty of the heroic struggle of righteousness against evil" (96). In the town's furor over "dirty books," Sopwith and little Tennessee Franklin, daughter of a Socialist and freethinker, stand by their ideals and both lose. Tennessee refuses to accept the imposed censorship; her father loses his job; both he and his daughter must leave Pompton. But when business interests begin to suffer from Sopwith's tyrannical censorship of books and vaudeville, the town also turns against him; and he too must leave a place where "people could comfortably profess one thing and do another . . ." (97).

As Dell's study shows, idealism does not always lead to truth, beauty, and goodness: sometimes they make man a tyrant, as with Sopwith; a rebellious martyr, as with Tennessee Franklin; a confused dreamer, as with Judith Valéntine; a fearful coward, as with Roy Sopwith, the principal's son. The love affair between Judith and Roy becomes a stormy episode in their pursuit of conflicting ideals.

Young Roy Sopwith has always wanted "to be an artist more than anything else in the world" (115). Unlike his sister, who has defied her father by going to Boston to become a journalist, Roy has been afraid of life until his meeting with Judith. Bolstered by a bit of money that he himself has earned, and finally by a job as house painter for old Mr. Cartwright, he asserts his independence. With a similar confidence of youthful rebellion, Judith finds a position on the town newspaper and discovers that her long exile ends with her interest and involvement in the town. Although she becomes only a spectator, the world of Pompton has begun to interest her; "She had begun to be relaxed and at ease among ordinary things" (158).

As she accepts Pompton, the town begins to accept both Judith and Roy as sweethearts. Frightened by the change that has come over her, Judith, neither alone, now, nor free, feels like a "fish caught in a net" (162). She rebels at Roy's contentment, his readiness to be caught by Pompton values; and, since she believes that they have lost their freedom to decide their future, she gives up any thought of marriage. She convinces Roy that he should strive to be an artist; she reminds herself to hold on to the dreams that have been part of her youth. If a passion for an ideal has led to marriage, the prospects of marrying and settling down in Pompton have revived an older ideal that seems the more important.

But what ideals *are* more important? Indeed, are ideals worthy of pursuit? Mr. Byington, editor of the *Patriot,* Judith's employer, answers these questions without being asked. At fifty-one, he has ceased to believe in much that he believed at nineteen. Once he had tried to be another Keats; now, as a "pillar of the community," he needs whiskey to get through the day. The trouble lies with ideals, and ideals "aren't so easy to chase away" (203). Whatever he has become, he knows that he isn't what he set out to be. "Life—not poetry," he tells Judith, is the important thing; and, as if to prove the point, Dell presents two examples: Miss Sickles, the society editor, who once wrote poetry, now settles for a cigarette smoked in secrecy after dinner; Hugo Massinger, would-be novelist, newspaper man, vagabond, whose idealism is only that of expediency: he took "every accident as a gift of the gods to their favourite child." Whatever charm Massinger has only wearies Judith, who knows that he will return to respectability and find it "rather wonderful, because it happened to him" (234). In following her own ideal, mad as it may be, her own dream, which has not brought happiness, has she made the right choice? If Janet March, who comes to terms with life, has, then Judith Valentine has not.

To understand the behavior and decision of Judith—and finally of Dell's meaning in the novel—is to realize that, as with the character of Felix Fay, Dell is not wholly sympathetic with his heroine. As the omniscient spectator, he dramatizes the story in clear, precise prose and without editorial comment. But the implications are always there: when people follow ideals for their own sake, when they fail to adjust their dreams to the business of real living—such people fail to realize their goals of freedom and happiness. But the adaptation must be real, not, as in the case of editor Byington, a verbal explanation that hides the unhappiness and maladjustment in his life. In a sense, Judith Valentine is simply running away, not to fulfill herself, but to preserve a youthful dream that she keeps confusing with rebellious assertion.

If neither heroine nor hero seems to achieve his or her ideal, perhaps Hugo Massinger comes nearest; for, after his crazy life, he reaches the sensible conclusion that ordinary things do count —a conclusion that Dell himself had reached long ago. In an era of disillusionment, Dell continued to believe in and admire the individual who could, as he said in *The Masses* in 1916, "buck up and refuse to let circumstances imprison [him] . . . in their accustomed way." In the context of his own belief, not unlike that of Browning's optimism and "psychological curiosity" in meeting the problems of life, the outcome of *This Mad Ideal* contains high irony: Judith should have comprehended, but did not; Hugo Massinger should not have done so, and did.

III   Runaway

By the early autumn of 1925, Dell published his second novel within the year, *Runaway*. The themes and ideas are not new, but the emphasis on "returning" is: *Runaway* is the story of Michael Shenstone, a vagabond-hero, whose flight from and return to the little town of Beaumont is, at the same time, the quest of the double-man who wants to "live always in the wide strange, disorderly universe," but who has tried and failed to settle down into a successful business in a "neatly-patterned world." In Beaumont, a place that Dell never precisely locates, the hero dreams of China; in China, he dreams of Beaumont and his only daughter Amber. Because of his desire to see her, he returns; and, while he comes back to a private world of memories and time past, to the age-old and mythical meaning of a jade dragon, he also returns to face a new world that includes his own daughter, his friends, the happenings in his own life, the little cottage and square of earth and trees. After the first chapter that describes the hero's history and flight, Dell's concern is not so much with the leaving as with the returning; and, since the return constitutes a new beginning, not a dead end, the major part of the novel describes the discoveries and adjustments that such a return entails.

In emphasizing the return "flight," Dell is not really breaking new ground. In the Felix Fay stories and in *Janet March* wandering is more a discovery than flight; and, in the use of flight image in describing Janet's ecstasy as "taking wings" and in punning on wings for the name of the village Winga Bay, Dell seems little more than poetic and amusing. In *Runaway,* even to a greater extent than in *This Mad Ideal,* where "flight" combines with "idealism" as aim and action, the image becomes integral to the title, to the theme, and to the thought and feeling of the characters; for it helps describe their actions and explain their inner thoughts. Just as flight may mean escape, rebellion, revolution, the pursuit of an ideal, or a runaway, so it may connote such opposite, yet related, meanings as return to nature, earth, art and to an ideal. Embracing both departure and return, the idea of flight for Dell includes a widening and deepening of man's consciousness; and the return often leads an individual back into the social matrix. Flight as both idea and image suggests freedom as well as limitation, growth as well as loss; it implies the process of maturation, the importance of art and creativity, the force and power of love.

In addition to the flight metaphor, Dell makes a greater use of image and symbol in *Runaway* than in his previous novels. In *Moon-Calf* and *The Briary-Bush,* of course, books, streets, and towns have symbolic significance; often the name of a village suggests a quality: Pompton in *This Mad Ideal* is pompous; Beaumont in *Runaway* is, but not at first, a beautiful place. But in *Runaway* the jade dragon, the drooping willow, even the act of running away and returning are integral to the moral and psychological meaning of the novel.

Thus, Michael Shenstone's return to Beaumont after seventeen years is, in itself, both a pilgrimage and a new beginning. Wearing the cloak, the hat, the beard that he wore in exile, he has not changed essentially from the vagabond he has always been: he has the "look of someone just arrived from Somewhere Else" (35). He has kept two things: the key to his cottage and his daughter's photograph. As if time has stood still, he finds the cottage just as he left it: the atlas is still open to the map of China, the whiskey barrel still contains a few drops of liquor, the willow tree outside still droops and moves. Nor has the town changed its opinion of him; he is still the runaway; and, if his reappearance provokes talk, it does not achieve his acceptance. Since he shows neither signs of repentance nor of prosperity, he remains an outcast. But, in returning to his past and to his daughter, he has also opened a new world for himself. The key has not only unlocked the old cottage but opened a way of accepting the ordinary things in life.

Although neither town nor Shenstone has changed its opinion of each other, their pasts remain inextricably tied together; as Dell demonstrates throughout the novel, individual lives make up the social fabric. Benjamin Chivers, the lawyer who was in love with Helena Shenstone before and after her husband left her, and who now looks after Amber Shenstone's estate, is part of that past which involves not only Shenstone and his daughter but also the estate money and the Ku Klux Klan. In a sense, Chivers' personal hatred for Shenstone hides behind a social and near-political organization that sneaks and skulks in the crevices of the town's social order. The hypocrisy of the Klan parallels the duplicity of Chivers' own life of respectability and furtive romance. Whatever influence he has had on Amber is somehow offset by the radical teachings, yet highly moral beliefs, of Victoria Wall, who has looked after Amber since the death of the girl's mother. Mrs. Wall, ". . . a pioneer in the struggle of her sex for freedom from ancient bondage" (43), is herself partly a stranger to Beaumont, but not to liberal truth: she has always represented Shenstone to Amber as "better, rather than worse, than the ordinary run of mankind" (48).

But Amber, who has prompted Shenstone's return, both revives the past and unites her father to the present; she meets him without malice and with few memories, but, at the same time, forces her father to consider his own motives. Indeed, the encounter serves as a mirror: he sees in Amber some of his own pride, his own petulance. As she tells him, "You are nothing to me! You are a stranger . . ." (59). But strangers can begin anew, as Dell implies, just as a younger generation, no longer tied to the past, can be deferential to Shenstone, not because he is scoundrel or saint, but because he is Amber's father.

Shenstone also learns something about man's need for making choices from people he meets. He understands how Amber may have been fascinated by the velvet jacket of Willy Ferenczi, Hungarian conductor of the town orchestra, and how she may have thought that marriage to him would give her romance and freedom and escape from Beaumont. In Dirk Tillinghast, a married man with whom Amber agrees to elope, Shenstone sees what might have happened to himself if he had stayed in Beaumont: a reporter on the *Banner,* a kind of Greenwich Village Swinburne, Tillinghast spins tales of the village where he had once lived and defied the Puritans by drinking bootleg booze. George Weatherby, a young lawyer in Beaumont, is even more significant in Shenstone's life, not because Amber finally marries the man but because Shenstone can actually give him something—the sympathy and understanding and compassion that Weatherby needs. The two men have much in common: in the past, Shenstone befriended the young Weatherby by reading some of the boy's poetry. Having grown up and become some-

thing of a runaway himself. Weatherby has been to college and
law school, served in the war, lived in Paris, but returned to
Beaumont to practice law. A little "shy and lonely," even "dis-
agreeably cynical," he has remained an alien presence in the
town, a disinterested observer. His "wry smile" and "curiosity"
are what remain of a man's youth gone sour. Modeled partly on
Dell and partly on Arthur Davison Ficke, Dell's lawyer-poet
friend and collector of Japanese prints, Weatherby shows what
happens to the runaway who has never quite resolved the "dark
unseen struggle" of his own life.

To understand Shenstone's decision to seek the trusteeship of
Amber's estate and in turn to expose Chivers and the Klan is to
comprehend Shenstone's—and Dell's—observations on the relation of individual to society. Shenstone's reminiscences about
his visit to the Orient are both philosophic and psychological:
"Living in the East sharpens your wits . . . and hardens . . . the
conscience. It gives you a deeper indifference to individual fate,
and a more profound respect for the essence of the human spirit" (123). In the East, conservatism means a fear of nature's anarchy, a respect for order. "At a loss if I tried to conform,"
Shenstone remembers Confucius' saying: "when the wall is too
high to climb over, there must be a crack to slip through" (123-
24). He seeks that crack. In the Orient, such a search is done with
candor; in Beaumont, with hypocrisy. In the Orient, he could
be his essentially selfish self; no one cared. His return makes him
feel the scoundrel that he has forgotten himself as being. His return is "not away from life's serious realities, but in among
them for a change" (126). But in becoming a scoundrel, in helping his daughter, and in opposing Chivers, he functions as a
social reformer and a personal savior.

The reconciliation of father and daughter—they break "through
the barrier of silence at last"—gives Shenstone insight not only
into their relationship but also into the meaning of the dragon
in their lives. He tells Amber: "You mustn't think of me as a
poetic vagabond. . . . Those are merely my airs. I like to impress
people, and I need to fool myself a little too" (148). His confessions explore the psychology of escape and flight: "If I was
looking for something at first, I've long since forgotten what it
was. Perhaps I learned that the thing I was looking for didn't

exist. But I had got into the habit of looking, and so I kept it up" (149). Rather, as he says, "I ran away from a certain kind of respectability, because I didn't like it. . ." (150). When he realizes that Amber has dreamed of him in much the same way that he himself had dreamed of China, he begins to recognize the power of the dragon's mystery: has it not seen into his heart? Has it not known the hunger of a "silly old man" for "the love that he did not deserve, the pride in the young happiness that he had done nothing to secure . . .?" (158). The dragon has enticed them both; those "strange, quaint, impossible, obscure and preposterous wishes" have ensnared them (162).

And this demon is both poison and medicine. Like art, it is the "sealing up, in some perfect phrase or some perfect shape, of these poisons of the human heart, to medicine sick hearts" (163). In breaking the dragon, Shenstone breaks not his belief in it but an attachment to it—to a dream that has dominated his vision, poisoned his perceptions, lured him into following an illusion. What he sees amounts to a glimpse of his true self: if he has thought that he ran away from his wife, he now realizes that she too was a rebel and that he had never "asked her to try her wings with him" (164). Actually, it was he who had become the respectable citizen of Beaumont; and, in running, he had run from himself, "had surrendered to the Beaumont part of himself—to his own foolish pride and shame . . ." (164). In breaking the dragon, he has broken a fixed idea that was never quite true.

Although Dell's use of the Klan parade is integral to the plot and characters of his novel, its function in the social life of the town receives sharp analysis. As George Weatherby says, the secret organization is composed of "morons and degenerates" and "simple-minded people—the corner grocer," who "likes to think of himself as a Nordic." The leaders are mostly "clever business men who are busy gathering in the ten-dollar bills and salting them away" (191). At present, the Klan is a front for bootleggers; and, if the night of revelry leaves murder and death in its wake, Chivers' confession reveals how he has appropriated Amber Shenstone's estate money.

The description of the Klan parade, the arrival of the state militia, and the defeat of Chivers is one of the most swift-moving episodes in any of Dell's novels. The action brings a reversal of roles: ruined, Chivers is the romantic, the criminal, who must leave town; Shenstone, the sensible man, correct even on financial matters, has become something of a hero. As he remarks, "the reclaimed sinner makes always the most popular saint" (250). Dell portrays the night of revelry partly through the thoughts of individuals as they view and react to events: through Pete Moss's woman friend from Kansas; the paranoiac young stablehand who fired the shot; through Weatherby, Amber, and Aunt Victoria.

The "outside" world has begun to accept Shenstone, but he accepts it (as did Dell) only insofar as his rebellious and critical mind allows; for he aligns himself politically with those of neither the far Right nor the far Left. To young Jim Pickett, who represents a new brand of self-styled Communist, militant, assertive, Shenstone's own career has but dramatized "the collapse of bourgeois morality" (171). Even if the muddled radicals admire him, Pickett does not: "Their radicalism consists merely in admiring disorder. They'll get in our way when we start to build up" (171). Shenstone observes:

I'm not worried about what he's going to do in the way of destruction. I'm all for it, to tell the truth. No, it's the reconstruction that my imagination boggles at. A world in the hands of sane, just, ruthlessly efficient young men like James Pickett! A world where everybody will get his three meals a day by working for them, and loafers will be shot at sunrise! What's to become of life's interesting variety? And that's not the worst. What will those stern young men do to art and literature? The censorship you have now . . . will be nothing to theirs. (177)

What Shenstone has learned—"what my old-fashioned and ironic mind was capable of taking in"—is that life is hard and that, while we need social planning, we also need art and love. Art— the Japanese prints—gives Shenstone his keenest insight into himself and into the world around him.

In the final scenes of the novel, which also unite Weatherby and Amber, Shenstone finds a solution that running away no longer gives. With insight partly shaped by the order he has always found in Japanese art, he sees that the corner of his yard is a "bit of the ancient East": the willow, the waterfall, the flower suggest the relationship and the forgetfulness to be found in nature and earth.

Dell's concluding statement, with its echoes of Jungian psychology, is both attitude and act. To Shenstone, the carved dragon has become "an image older than the conscious memory of the race." It is "the image of something beautiful and terrible, —outside of man's sane hopes, yet inexorably a part of man's destiny,—sometimes darkly hostile and sometimes inscrutably consoling. An enigma, like man himself" (303-4). Man's central and abiding problem, whether vagabond, artist, or father, remains that of adapting himself to the social, political, and economic world in which he lives.

Shenstone's involvement with social and political elements is as close as Dell comes to incorporating the current social and political scene into his novels. He had not lost interest in the need for social reorganization or in revolutionary tactics, but, just as the young activist was unable to help Shenstone, Dell himself found that his choice led him to the more fundamental problem of man's need to adjust with integrity to the new and changing world in which all perforce must live. Rebellion had made Shenstone a vagabond; and vagabondage had brought chaos, disillusionment, and the substitution of one tyranny for another. If rebellion remains still a necessary step, man must finally return, therefore, to concepts of law and order. Only from such vantage points can ideals function as sensible goals; only then can freedom, beauty, love, truth be glimpsed, not as abstract theory, but as workable creative truths.

Shenstone's return to nature is the return to an order that is more universal and enduring than any political creed or tyrannical act. Dell called *Runaway* a slight novel, but in it he has explored with clarity and dramatic intensity the personal-social conflict in his own life, one that in one way or another touches the lives of many. During the 1920's his own social and political thinking will clash openly with the growing militancy of the revolutionary Left.

Reflecting on the early novels in pages of *Homecoming* that were never included in the published version, Dell wrote that he "forgot for a time that I was writing, in my novels, a 'contemporary History of the Breakdown of the Patriarchal Family'."[11]

But it seemed to him then that *Moon-Calf, The Briary-Bush, Janet March*—even *This Mad Ideal*—

accidentally or not, did actually illustrate the decay of parental authority under stress of machine-age economic conditions, together with the independence of youth, the rebellion of girls, and the beginnings, in painful but educative emotional experiment, of a natural kind of marriage, the marriage of the future. Somewhere within that cycle of novels would be one dealing with the position of the poet or artist, who in our society, as in the past, is seriously discouraged from the assumption of ordinary sexual responsibilities, and must often renounce either poetry or the obligation of marriage.[12]

But to write the kind of novels that he wanted to write he had a price to pay. With the suppression of *Janet March,* "the struggle with poverty," he said, "had begun for me." Since sales of the novels had fallen, they no longer supported him; and, in order to pay "the grocer and butcher." he continued to supplement his income by writing stories and articles.

Having finished *Runaway* in 1925, Dell and his family made their only trip to Europe. Leaving in May, they spent ten weeks in London. Dell did research in the British Museum on Robert Burton's *The Anatomy of Melancholy,* while living in the "Maisonette" of his old friend Charles Hallinan of the Chicago *Post* days, now a London journalist. They met friends—Julian Huxley, Frank Swinnerton, Crystal Eastman; but Dell did not like London: "it reeked . . . of a hateful past." Besides, he became severely ill with gastritis.

In Paris, which the Dells liked better than London, they lived on the Left Bank near the Luxembourg Gardens. When Dell recovered a bit, he visited the cathedral at Chartres; but it did not reconcile him to the Middle Ages. At the French Riviera, which he called an American suburb, they met many people they knew; but Dell was still sick and miserable. In September, he was happy to return to his home in Croton, where he continued to recuperate and began to plan a number of new projects.

CHAPTER *6*

Dell as Essayist and Critic

ALTHOUGH Dell continued to write novels throughout the 1920's, his career as editor, reviewer, essayist, and literary historian had not yet ended. Still an editor of *The Liberator* in 1920 and a contributor to other magazines, he readied a number of writings for publication: by the end of the 1920's, he had brought out two volumes of one-act plays, most of them written in the Greenwich Village days; three collections of essays and reviews; a study in literary history; and a newly written critical analysis of the writings of Upton Sinclair. He edited small volumes of the writings of Wilfred Scawen Blunt, Robert Herrick, William Blake, John Reed; and, with Paul Jordan-Smith, he prepared a new edition of Burton's *The Anatomy of Melancholy.* With Thomas Mitchell, Dell collaborated in converting one of his novels into a successful Broadway play. But there were changes, especially in his position as editor.

The Liberator, as Daniel Aaron points out, had "continued the battle for art and socialism"; and, for a while, it had maintained much of the same fun-loving charm and inconsistency as its predecessor, *The Masses,* with an editorial point of view that still reflected both Bohemian and revolutionary attitudes. Eastman's "pro-Bolshevik harangues," Aaron notes, "contrasted oddly with Floyd Dell's praise of G. K. Chesterton's war against the servile state. . . ."[1] But the split in thinking that had beset *The Liberator* staff—Eastman said it went back to 1916—became more and more apparent. The division, Eastman explains in *Love and Revolution,* was "between the emotional true believers and the thinking minds, the adherents of a faith and the participants in an effort." If one wants freedom, such a division, he thought, was even more important than "that between economic classes." The war against any idea or a set of fixed ideas was essential to the character of a magazine. Actually, the war against capitalism belongs "to a brief period in history." The "war for moral, intellectual and aesthetic freedom . . . is eternal."[2] Clearly, Eastman and Dell stood in the liberal-individual tradition of Shaw and Wells; but Mike Gold, who joined the staff in January, 1921, was a militant, emotional believer in the tradition of Upton Sinclair and Jack London. When the conflict began, the differing attitudes of Dell and Gold became a center of controversy.

Michael Gold (Irwin Granich), who had grown up in the slums of the East Side of New York, began making his revolutionary convictions felt through magazine articles and speeches. One debate with Dell about free love versus marriage was the fourth in a series of *Liberator* "Evening Affairs" in 1922. Opposite in temperament, in background, and in method and manner of being revolutionary, Gold and Dell continued to disagree openly and privately throughout the decade. Clearly something of the old *Masses-Liberator* unity had been lost, and Joseph Freeman writes that the "new group," including Gold and Claude McKay, Negro poet and contributor to the magazine, "did not yet have the stature of the old," of John Reed, Eastman, and Dell; and that the "organized punch of the old journal was gone."[3]

Although individual contributions to *The Liberator* were of high quality and the circulation continued largely unchanged, the magazine began to suffer from discord and from a shifting editorial staff. In March, 1921, when Crystal Eastman stepped down as managing editor, Eastman, Dell, Robert Minor, and Claude McKay took over as joint editors. The arrangement was, at best temporary; and years later, in his appreciation of Dell in *Love and Revolution,* Eastman remembers Dell's many capabilities and wonders why he "did not offer to leave the magazine in his accomplished hands." Dell's gift for "falling in with, and exquisitely judging, the writings of others," as well as his capacities for political argument on several sides of a question, made him uniquely valuable to the magazine.[4] Busy with his novels, Dell probably would not have accepted the position; but he joined with the others, as Eastman wrote, in making *The Liberator* more like *The Masses* in spirit, and "in subject-matter a little more closely related to the American labor movement."[5] Then, in October, 1921, E. F. Mylius (really Edward Boskin), bookkeeper for the magazine, absconded with forty-five hundred dollars of *Liberator* funds, just as he was being dismissed as a measure of economy.

Shortly after this incident, there were other staff changes. With a continued zeal for "rabid revolution," Mike Gold wanted the magazine to become even more militant. Eager to be freed of the editorship and to go to Europe, Eastman suggested that Gold take over. When Gold and Claude McKay became executive editors, Dell remained as one of seven editors and served on the board of directors. By June, McKay, unable to work with Gold, resigned; and Joseph Freeman, who had joined the staff in the summer of 1922, became associate editor with Gold. This arrangement lasted until August, when Dell replaced Gold for the October, 1922, issue; Dell was, in turn, replaced by Robert Minor, who, with Joseph Freeman, became the executive editors. Although Dell "had already begun his self-imposed exile in the suburbs," as Freeman put it, he stayed on as "art" editor until the last issue in October, 1924, when the magazine combined with *The Labor Herald* and with *The Soviet Russia Pictorial* to become *The Workers Monthly.*

In the final issue of 1924, *The Liberator* published the last and fifteenth installment of Dell's essay, "Literature and the Machine Age"; and Robert Minor, still editor, was hopefully announcing that in the next issue "Floyd Dell will continue his brilliant work which has become so vital a part of the life-blood of *The Liberator.*"[6] Minor's judgment of Dell's contribution to the magazine was right, but the end had come: the magazine that Dell and Eastman had conceived and edited had been absorbed by the political activists. Actually, despite his devotion to social causes, to reforms and rebellion, Dell remains the independent revolutionary—the radical thinker, unique and alone.

I   *The Personal Revolutionary*

By the early 1920's Dell was already well-known in intellectual circles not only in Chicago and New York but also in the nation and in Europe. As editor and reviewer he had, in one way or another, come in contact with the leading writers and thinkers of his time; many of them he knew personally; many he could number as firsthand, if not intimate, acquaintances; with many he had worked on the magazine and in the theater. Since coming to *The Masses* in 1913, he had, by the mid-1920's, been an inspiriting and influential thinker and participant for more than ten years—nearly fifteen, counting the time in Chicago—in the social, political, literary, and intellectual life of his time. When H. G. Wells came to New York in the winter of 1921-22, he asked especially to meet Floyd Dell.

One of Dell's most articulate admirers was Joseph Freeman. Along with other young radicals at Columbia University in 1916 and following World War I, Freeman looked on Dell as one of those who helped form "the cult of the Universal Man." Although he and Dell did not actually meet until 1921, Freeman had, as he recalls, "followed his writings regularly, and considered them a source of Wisdom, like the writings of other men personally unknown to me, Francis Bacon or Thomas Paine, who nevertheless were my teachers." Freeman admired Dell's courage to differ with acknowledged masters, to praise unknown writers, to see and use a "social approach to books." In reviewing Dreiser's *The Genius* Dell had, Freeman writes, "reproached Dreiser for missing the chief point about his hero who was in essence a rebel. Life at its best and most heroic, Dell said, was rebellion; Dreiser was himself a rebel; why did he not write the American novel of rebellion? . . . He made it clear that a writer could not escape his social responsibilities by hiding behind the skirts of art."[7] As articulated in a single review, Dell's position seems simple and clear-cut, easily grasped and understood.

Yet, as his writings reveal, Dell's personality and thinking were paradoxical and complex. Like the heroes and heroines of his novels, Dell has much of the double-man about him: he is the withdrawn individualist and the would-be participating observer; he is the shy, "moon-calf" dreamer, whose ideas and attitudes are militantly aggressive. In protesting some social evil or political idea, he can bring the force of his wit, the strength of his learning; but his treatment of his subject through the "detached observer" and his use of irony, with its inherent strategy of shifting back and forth between meanings, always make it difficult to pin him down. Surely he leans toward rebellion and socialism, toward revolution and freedom; but he is always the artist, not the militant activist, the artist whose mode of action is best realized through his writing.

As Eastman says, speaking of the early days of *The Liberator,* Dell "was adding a humanistic-essay flavor to the revolutionary gospel that was forever after sadly missing."[8] What Dell had achieved was an accretion of thought and experience: he was shy, rebellious, the Socialist; an admirer of Emerson, Browning, Whitman; a mad idealist; a worker of extraordinary energy, generous, humorous; a Village sophisticate; but he was never far from his radical beginnings in the Illinois villages and towns where he had grown up; he had remained close to earth and to nature.

Unlike many American writers and artists who had left New York for Paris or London, Dell had gone no farther than Croton-on-Hudson. With a kind of open-door policy and friendly generosity, as Freeman remembers, Dell became "father confessor to dozens of moon-calves" to whom he gave time, energy, even "literary and material help." The conversation was brilliant, although Dell was never fond of "repartee and the short sally." Only after the smalltalk had dribbled away and a general problem had presented itself did Dell take over: "Then he would cross-examine a guest by the Socratic method, and finally, like Socrates, launch forth on a long monologue."[9]

Dell had always loved talk, but he now saw, as Clive Bangs said in *The Briary-Bush,* that there was something "hopelessly old-fashioned" about it. Unconventional as his generation had been, it had also "stopped on the way to discuss the matter more thoroughly, and ended by never doing anything at all."[10] But what is "hopelessly old-fashioned" about Dell's feelings and prejudices is also very hopefully and sensibly American. As he said in 1920, his generation was one of "idealists and lovers of beauty and aspirants toward freedom," who felt themselves during the "long years of their youth . . . in solitary conflict with a hostile environment. . . ." They were also sturdy individualists; and, as he observed, we "brooded too long apart to become without pain a part of the social group to which we belong."[11] Compared, then, to the narrow-minded, militant young men of action, Dell surely seemed wrong, inconsistent, weak, a renegade. Actually, whatever his inconsistencies and contradictions, they came from the breadth and depth of the larger, more personal vision toward which he was impelled.

II   Looking at Life

Long before *The Liberator* ceased publication, Dell had already begun to collect some of his writings—the Village plays, reviews, and critical essays—for book publication. Three comedies, *King Arthur's Socks* (1916), *The Angel Intrudes* (1918), and *Sweet and Twenty* (1921) had been separately published before Dell brought them out in 1922 as part of a single volume of eleven one-act plays, entitled *King Arthur's Socks and Other Village Plays.* "They are," he writes in the prefatory note, "souvenirs of an intellectual play-time which, being dead, deserves some not-too-solemn memorial." With the exception of *Poor Harold,* performed by the Mount Airy Players in 1920, the plays date from the 1913-18 period, and were performed either at the old Liberal Club or by the Provincetown Players in the Village. Dell had acted in some of them and so had Edna Millay, Eastman, and George Cram Cook.

Looking at Life, Dell's third volume of essays, appeared in 1924. Both *Women as World Builders* and *Were You Ever a Child?* had been built around a single theme; but the forty essays in *Looking at Life,* more than half of which had appeared in *The Masses* and in *The Liberator,* contain a variety of subjects that include feminism, censorship, national manners and customs. There are essays on books, literary, and political topics, including the essay-reviews on Chesterton's and Bertrand Russell's political ideas. In some of the essays insignificant changes have been made: "Sherwood Anderson, his First Novel" appeared in *The Masses* as "A New American Novelist." Such essays as "Lost Paradise," which appeared as "Greenwich Village," and "Not without Dust and Heat," which had appeared as "The Story of the Trial," were slightly revised. All of the essays had appeared within a ten-year period—from 1914 to 1923—and were, with one exception, arranged by year with a kind of topical sequence. For whatever reason, Dell had selected more essays from 1916 and 1919 than from any other years.

More than half of the essays in *Looking at Life* are on writers, many of them his favorites—Shaw, Whitman, Whittier, Wells, Housman. With typical Dellian clarity and candor, he reminds Jean Starr Untermeyer that she fails to celebrate the "spiritual enfranchisement of your sex." He praises Sandburg for his "queer tune" and "the things you sing about" and McFee for his ability to make interesting the "lives of two ordinary people"; Anderson for his fearless, candid ability as an "interpreter of American life." Often impressionistic, Dell also analyzes a writer's contribution to the age. Maintaining his own critical point of view, he does so in language that is free from ideological cant and jargon. Some of the essays—on Greenwich Village, the first *Masses* trial, the review of Housman's poetry—are chiefly autobiographical. But his most sustained examples of literary criticism are found in two succeeding volumes, in *Intellectual Vagabondage* and in the study of Upton Sinclair.

III   Intellectual Vagabondage

Intellectual Vagabondage, An Apology for the Intelligentsia was published in March, 1926. Dell had written the essay in 1919; revised it for *The Liberator* in 1923-24, where it appeared as "Literature and the Machine Age"; and then expanded it slightly for his book. His general theme is the relation between life and literature; he sets out to look "at the role which the intelligentsia has played in times past" and to expose the weaknesses and follies of his generation of intellectuals. As Dell sees it, their literary record of "pain, chagrin, disgust, cynicism, defeat, and failure," may give a new generation little help, either in understanding life or in living it in "larger, freer, braver, more beautiful and significant ways than it was lived in the past . . ." (xiii). Actually, the "most characteristic literature" of his own generation, as Dell sees it, has failed; and he announces his intention "to tell the whole truth about our generation by way of explanation and apology" (xiii). His defense is both indictment and justification; and, while written in the pluralistic "we," it is both autobiography and literary history.

In what Dell calls "the first attempt in America to apply a particular principle of historical criticism to any wide range of literary productions,"[12] Dell defines literature as a record, often "in strange symbols and fantasies and fictions," of the "significant stages in the history of what men and women have thought and felt" about the meaning of the endless struggle of man with a changing environment. As he writes, "A significant writer is a person whose conscious emotions correspond to the deep unexpressed feelings of others, and whose candor and courage and sheer writing ability are adequate to the task of expressing these feelings, so that he becomes their spokesman" (22).

As for the identity of these spokesmen and the sequence of thinking that brought a whole generation to a feeling of alienation and social hopelessness, Dell is quite specific. Beginning with Defoe, he illuminates the writer-intellectual's role with swift, incisive strokes; and he selects writers that have had meaning for him personally and that have frequently appeared in his novels in the role of "teacher." As a clear-cut statement of the revolutionary idea that any man can do his own fighting, plowing, and governing, *Robinson Crusoe* embodies the wishes, hope, and dreams of the young trading class of the eighteenth century. Rousseau's voice against restriction had given impetus to men's ideals, but the promises ended in despair; the rule of reason became the Reign of Terror. The Romantic writers fled, "seeking with morbid fondness those far and solitary peaks, glaciers, caverns, seas, deserts, which constitute the favorite milieu of early nineteenth-century poetry" (49). Some literally fled the deadly machine-world of England for the joys of travel. Some, like Carlyle, found salvation in "great men," and in the medieval world. Others, like Dickens and Thackeray, turned to "literary Grand Opera," or found, like De Quincey, new interest in "verbal effects."

The impact of the new science only intensified the response of the writer to his environment, for man began to discover "at the very basis of the scheme of life the hated conditions of the new capitalistic order—the life-and-death struggle between more and less fortunately equipped individuals" (82-83). The real issue of the Darwinian controversy lay in the doctrine of natural selection, which put the emphasis, not on origin, but on process, and which, in the popular mind, became the cause of evolutionary change and of all progress in general. Darwin's descriptions became doctrine: "Each man for himself and the devil take the hindmost" (83). The response to a new environment varies: Meredith, for instance, sees man betrayed by an inner falseness, which a return to earth and nature can hopefully redeem; Hardy, examining the universal processes of nature and the whims of gods, finds more doom than hope in the world. Others, like the esthetes, "thrown back upon a belief in themselves," find "their own personal lives devoid of significance" (99). They have reached the "last frontier of literature, the stepping-off place into the realm of madness—of private and incommunicable dream" (102). Whether the writer is forced "to be cut off from community of thought with the world to which one belongs," or whether he chooses to alienate himself and to try to escape, the results are equally disastrous.

In Part II, Dell addresses himself to the "spiritual autobiography of my own generation in its literary and social aspects" —"of those who wandered, seeking understanding of themselves and of the mysteries of life" (118). Actually, imaginative literature from the past had neither "borne the test of experience" nor made the searchers feel that they should even make the "effort to reshape this sorry scheme of things entire" (175). But some writers helped them find their way: Jules Verne interpreted the triumphs of science; Bob Ingersoll helped them with Darwin; Emerson and Thoreau, with their self-reliance; Whittier and Whitman, with their libertarian thinking. The gospel of the *Rubaiyat* taught them the endurance of pain and pleasure; Ibsen helped them to see the false pomposity of masculine superiority; in turn, the seekers also came to understand that women were already in industry and could be good companions. An interest in oppression became an interest in mankind at large, "in practical efforts, in politics and economics, for the relief of the world-wide misery produced by capitalism" (144).

But most of the generation, Dell believes, did not think a Great Change possible. They trusted the evolutionary process, the milder programs of reform: trust-busting, arbitration, profit-sharing, municipal ownership, organized charity. If the process led to a state trust, it also led to a disbelief in state; but the old theory of man's natural goodness emerged through syndicalism, guild socialism, and militant communism. And, when they searched for "authority" that would help them forget their fears of the state, they found it in psychology, which restored their "ego, lonely and triumphant," even freed them from the ghosts of public censure, tradition, and customs.

In consequence, as Dell points out, some intellectuals follow-ed the cult of the vagabond in a prolonged holiday away from life itself. Some became supervagabonds, seeing the world sim-ply as spectacle and using art as if it were religion. But to some, the world was made suddenly real. Wells and Shaw both helped them to "understand ourselves in relation to something besides our individual ambitions and our individual miseries" (225-26). Wells made them feel as if they were creators of the future, al-though the creating was to be done, not "with the help of any organized body, scientific, political, or economic," but by the individual himself. Thus, they were still confirmed in the impor-tance of their egotistic personalities. Shaw raised a disturbing question about the future: *"Can you create a new civilization upon the ruins of the old? Can you even get along in such a new civilization if some one else creates it for you?"* (233).

What, then, of the future? World War I had shattered man's idealism; and, with the prospects of "more gigantic and more destructive and more futile wars to come," many of the intel-ligentsia retreated into a new ivory tower and to a preoccupa-tion with form; others celebrated "the ugliness and chaos of life," dealing at least with meaning and events (240-42). Some turned to the unconscious, exploring the crevices of the mind, as if "we, at this moment in history, do *not* want life to seem capable of being interpreted and understood, because that would be a reproach to us for our own failure to undertake the task of reconstructing our social, political and economic theo-ries, and in general, and in consonance with these, our ideals of a good life" (249).

Dell's conclusions, radical and revolutionary, bear the stamp of his hope: the intelligentsia must formulate acceptable con-ventions, especially in the areas of love and marriage; find polit-ical means that will enable them to "accept and serve and use a machine civilization"; nourish the arts "as means of communi-cation rather than merely opportunities for irresponsible self-expression" (260). Whatever Dell's inconsistencies and inadequa-cies as a member of the very group he criticizes and defends, he concludes that the value of literature lies in helping man "to love generously, to work honestly, to think clearly, to fight bravely, to live nobly. . ." (260-61). It may seem strange that he thought of these as Communist virtues, but it was in 1920 that he thought so. Even so, such virtues lie squarely within the liberal American tradition.

Dell's attitude in *Intellectual Vagabondage* is not so much new direction as new assertion. The book is, he wrote later, "a repudiation of the Social Revolutionary and Anarchist philosophy, and by implication, though perhaps less clearly, an acceptance of the Communist philosophy."[13] If he had given such ideas currency for many years, nowhere else had he so ordered them as a historical account or given them sequential development. Because of Dell's easy and graceful phrasing, his book has a subtlety of argument and an ironic twist in statement that demand careful attention from a reader. The book is an apology for his generation; and, while Dell believes in change, he is no vagabond. He argues for freedom, but he recognizes its limits. He affirms his belief in revolution, but he also believes in order. He is a poet of youth and beauty, but he is no ivory-tower artist. He is interested in social and political reforms, but not in exchanging one tyranny for another. He supported the Russian revolution, World War I (and later World War II), and the Feminist movement; but Dell was never a blind devotee to some unexamined cause. If rebellion and revolution were to some a religion, to Dell they remained an essential part of the process of relating his ideals and his conception of a better life to the reality of living. What he saw as mysterious process, others tried to make into a program with a timetable. Whether Bohemian, Socialist, revolutionist, artist, editor, or novelist, Dell operated as a free and independent being—as the individual who, whatever the group within which he worked, stood quite firmly on his own moral and intellectual integrity.

IV   Love in Greenwich Village

Only a few weeks after the publication of *Intellectual Vagabondage, Love in Greenwich Village,* a collection of essays, stories, and poems which had already appeared in magazines, was published in mid-May, 1926. As with previous collections of re-printed items, Dell made only minor changes and revisions. The essays on the rise and fall of the Village, which had appeared in the October and November, 1925, issue of *The Century Magazine* as a single two-part essay, became the first and last essays in the volume. The subtitles, which had been used in the magazine, were omitted in the book; and sometimes a semicolon became a dash, or a dash a comma. Mostly, items remained unchanged. Dell had chosen material that, often dramatic in content, portrayed the feelings and emotions of those Villagers who found life a bittersweet affair.

Since by the mid-1920's a new Village had already replaced the one Dell first knew, *Love in Greenwich Village* is partly history, telling more about the past than the present. As history, the reader expects and sometimes finds an explicit use of factual and historical material, but in most cases Dell has changed the names of people—usually not places—so that what may have been actual events and happenings to actual people take on an air of fiction. Later he clarified in *Homecoming* some of the references, so that a reader can return to *Love in Greenwich Village* and make fairly accurate guesses—but even so, when Dell recalls actual names, he seldom elaborates on the episode; and, when giving details of the episode, he continues to omit names. Much of the meaning of the story-essays in *Love in Greenwich Village* lies in the tone or mood that envelopes the life and loves of those people described.

Actually, the volume is mostly personal, with an authenticity of thought and feeling that springs from Dell's own remembered experience as he recaptures the ghosts of "those lost, happy years," and of a place which had been the home mostly of young artists, who had loved their hopes and dreams as much as each other, and who had been willing to help one another and to live and love together, but not—for a while—to marry.

As the title might suggest, love takes on a variety of meanings and leads to a number of complications: in "The Kitten and the Masterpiece," both young artists fall in love with a little kitten and with each other; but both are also in love with writing their "masterpiece" and with the joy of loving. In "Phantom Adventure," Dell shows how "fiction" can be accepted but fact can-

not. When a banker wants to confess his adventure in love to his
wife, he tells the story as a story; and his wife, understanding
the real truth of it, is moved to tears. The nearest he can come
to truth is to tell his story to a writer, who, writing it as fiction,
can sell it to other dreamers. "The Button" tells of the frustration of a girl's love for her old life in the Village and of her
marriage. She returns to her husband but vows she can live a
double life.

"The Gifts of the Fourth Goddess" is a parable of how three
goddesses of the dim past become for a while Liberty, Equality,
and Fraternity; but, when their popularity wanes, they become
three old women and live in the Catskills. When a sculptor needs
statues of Wisdom, Truth, Mercy, and Justice, the old women
volunteer to serve as the first three; and they are joined by Miss
Wilkinson, dean of a girl's college, who becomes the fourth goddess. To future poetess, Pat Flower, they bring gifts at her chris-
tening: as Titania, one brings laughter; as Psyche, one brings curiosity and suffering; as Melusina, one brings the desire to be
human and know mortal love; Miss Wilkinson brings a sense of
social responsibility, respect for custom, and fear of making herself ridiculous. In Greenwich Village, poetess Pat Flower serves
that fourth goddess by kindling the pagan spirit, which means
something to Philistia—"all the beautiful things we want to do,
and can't. . . ." To break her engagement means to remain the
goddess she has become and to accept the love she receives.

In "Hallelujah, I'm a Bum," which is told against a background of the class struggle, the hero, a tramp, a criminal, a fu-
gitive from justice, finds love for a little while in the Village. "A
Piece of Slag," a story of free love, shows that in real life such
love is not always gay; rather, life itself has little form: it is
"crude, dirty, brutal, real, a piece of slag!" In "The Ex-Villager's
Confession," the practice of free love is a way to learn that
which would never have been believed from books.

As Dell looks back on his days in the Village, he concludes
that he and his friends had a "miraculous naïveté, a Late-Victo-
rian credulousness, a faith, happy and absurd, in the goodness
and beauty of this chaotic universe" (320-21). *Love in Greenwich Village* is filled with nostalgia, but in casting a faintly romantic glow on memories of a bygone era, it succeeds in con-

veying the innocence and ingenuousness of those who lived
and loved there.

V   Upton Sinclair

Love in Greenwich Village elegizes a way of life that, always
fun and exciting, involved both love and work. *Upton Sinclair,
A Study in Social Protest,* published in July, 1927, praises a social propagandist, whose life was mostly all work. Dell, who disagreed with Sinclair on many issues, felt that he was "one of the
leaders of a significant American literary movement" who was
being neglected by all but the Socialist press (187). Sinclair read
and checked the manuscript before publication, and some of
his comments appear as footnotes.

Sinclair, said Dell, belonged to "the race of giants." Although
other writers "may be more acute psychologists, .wiser in the
lore of human nature, more able to analyze and dramatize the
traditional passions of mankind," no other writer, Dell thought,
had given us such an account "of what America is in its most
characteristic contemporary aspects" (11-12). Sketching rather
briefly Sinclair's early years—his life of poverty, his struggle
through law school, his devotion to poetry, his career as hack
writer, his first marriage, his turn to socialism as an ideal by
which to live—Dell analyzes Sinclair's faults and virtues with
all the respect due a great writer.

More prewar Socialist than postwar Communist, Sinclair had
been and still was an outspoken social critic. With money from
his famous *The Jungle,* he had founded the ill-fated Helicon
Home Colony; but, when the house burned, he was without
funds. His health was poor; he was beset by domestic difficulties. After his return from Holland and remarriage, he had
turned to what Dell calls "pamphleteering." In his studies of
religion, journalism, education, literature, and economics, Sinclair rose to the "height of his powers." In describing human
and personal elements with scientific rigor, he achieved at his
best, Dell writes, "the narrative and dramatic and psychological
excitements of the novel" (161). Here he has come to "grips
with the American theme." Some of these same qualities are in
Oil: "if he can continue in this masterful way, not even his So-

cialist preoccupations can prevent him from being recognized as America's greatest novelist" (179).

Dell's admiration for Sinclair was of long standing. Joseph Freeman—to whom the study is dedicated—recalls that Dell saw himself as "a link in the Socialist literary tradition between Upton Sinclair and my generation," just as Freeman felt that his generation was a link "between the generation of Dell, Reed, and Minor and our juniors."[14] In the conversations that they had in 1925, Freeman remembers that Dell was calling for "social revolutionary criticism." Dell himself writes: ". . . how many first-rate writers are there who have not been social rebels?" Agreeing with Sinclair's attack on the "art-for-art's sake" theory, Dell concludes that bankruptcy of the "purely esthetic" point of view makes "social revolutionary criticism" an inevitable method. He defines it in his own voice:

> an artist is an interpreter of life, and judges the truth and value of his interpretation by the test of how fully he shows himself aware of what is going on in his world, with special reference to social change, and whether he helps his audience to understand and sympathize with such changes. He is recognized as a discriminator of spiritual values, in some sense a creator of them, and he is judged by the spiritual values he helps to create in a world that struggles toward something greater and finer than its past. He is not asked to be consciously attempting to create such values, and least of all is he asked to believe in this or that specific program of change—he is judged as an artist and not as a politician. It is a frankly partisan criticism, but it represents the genuine esthetic response of those who feel themselves to be living in a changing world lighted by the hope of revolutionary improvement. (174)

Sinclair seldom deals with erotic themes, as if, Dell interprets, such problems seem "to him . . . to be too involved with social problems to be isolated, and . . . too complex to be satisfactorily solved by mankind except upon terms of profound social change." With the "impatience of a revolutionary mind," Sinclair would not be "content with such tawdry or cruel or cowardly escapes as the world has thus far afforded to its rebels in the sexual realm" (176). These problems of artistic and social rebellion, of love, marriage, and erotic escapes, are some of the very problems in Dell's own life; and many of his friends and critics found his ideas and actions hard to reconcile. His nostalgia for Greenwich Village, his praise of the social revolutionary, and his highly critical comments of the social and literary scene helped to make him a target in the changing life of the 1920's.

By September 30 Dell's new novel—*An Unmarried Father*—was ready for publication; and on December 23, 1927, Doran published a limited edition of Robert Burton's *The Anatomy of Melancholy,* which Dell and Paul Jordan-Smith had edited. For the first time, Burton's text appeared all in English; the many Latin quotations were translated so as to "restore to this work the unhindered appreciation which it had in its author's own day." Both editors signed the preface; each contributed a part of the introduction. Dell, who sees Burton as a precursor of Freud, notes that this other psychologist's attention to the unreasonable part of man's mind is not unlike a similar interest in the "unreasonable part of man's mind" today.

VI   The New Masses

In 1923 the committee for *The Bookman* magazine selected Dell as an outstanding novelist of what was called "The Younger Group." Praised as "a careful workman, a close student of psychology, a sympathetic observer of the facts of life, a fearless realist," Dell is, the article continues, "as earnest and hard working a figure as one remembers in contemporary American writing."[15] Dell's continued output during the 1920's surely attests the accuracy of judgment. The quarrel lay with Dell's changed point of view, with what many of his friends and critics believed were unforgivable inconsistencies: he had talked rebellion and practiced free love, and now he had settled down in the suburbs as a happily married man. Actually, of course, the problem of change was far more complex than a quarrel with any one person; but the quarrel with Dell epitomized the old and continuing quarrel that had beset *The Liberator* over political, social, and literary thinking. That quarrel was soon intensified in the pages of the *New Masses.*

Appearing in May, 1926, the *New Masses* seemed at first as gaudily ideal as its old predecessor and given to as much freedom in matters of art and sex. But, under the editorship of Mike Gold and Joseph Freeman, and with considerable pressure from readers and workers and whatever foreign sources, the policy

began to shift in favor of artworks that celebrated the worker-
hero and the proletariat in their social and political struggles. In
the proletariat, Gold reminded them, the "real conflicts of men
and women" were to be found, not in the "silly little agonies"
of a sickly, sentimentalized Bohemian adventure. With mission-
ary-like zeal, Gold exhorted and admonished artists to stop the-
orizing; to admit that individualism led to cliques and eccen-
tricities; and to seek an active part in the life of their times,
both literally and artistically. As Daniel Aaron points out, "the
leftward turn of the American intelligentsia" that took place
between 1928 and 1931 was underway.

When the *New Masses* appeared, Dell was listed as one of the
contributing editors; but his differences with Mike Gold had, as
we have noted, long been pronounced and public. In *The Liberator* days they had quarreled openly: Gold might think he is a
member of the working class, Dell had written in 1922, but he
was really a "literary man, an intellectual, and a member of the
salaried middle class."[16] No one needed to be ashamed of such
status, Dell had argued; for most artists were not organizers any-
way, and were doing what they chose and could do best: writing
better articles or drawing better pictures. Moreover, no one
needed to be ashamed of leisure: if it were so "glorious to work
twelve hours a day . . . there would be no need of a revolutionary movement in this country." Dell agreed that he did not
want to become like the miners; he wanted something better for
them. Answers and criticisms were, of course, forthcoming. As
Aaron points out, "The assault against Dell as the disagreeable
anti-hero, the radical corrupted, was carried on by Gold and the
spiritual sons of John Reed with increasing bitterness after
1926."[17]

When V. F. Calverton, editor of the Marxist *Modern Quarterly,* joined the attack, he accused Dell of both withdrawing and
selling out. In summarizing Dell's explanation, Aaron points out
that Dell had tried, and was still trying, to solve the conflict between his narcissistic and social impulses, and that, while he accepted communism and saw no "contradiction between his new
concern for education, sex, and the family and the realities of
the Soviet state," he was less able to celebrate in fiction the present effort to achieve Communist rule in America than he was

to describe the machine-age. And, while he could detect "the neurotic origins of much political radicalism," he chose not to satirize it, as he could have done, out of loyalty to the radical cause.[18] In *Upton Sinclair,* Dell, discussing how artists needed to cope with the theme of "modern industrial America," points out that he believed such pamphleteering as Sinclair was doing furnished "a pattern, an ideological map of the scene" even "perhaps the experimental models of a fiction soon to be born, able to cope with such a theme as America presents" (162).

But Calverton was not to be dissuaded. In April, 1929, writing in the *New Masses,* he declared that "intellectuals, on the whole, are so superficial that their revolt is seldom revolutionary." Among others, he specifically mentions Dell, who, "with a genius for style" and a "fine understanding of the philosophic aspects of radical reconstruction," has alienated himself further and further from it, surrendering to "commercial creation" and writing fiction that has "neither deep meaning nor challenging significance."[19]

Within a month (May 23, 1929) Dell had resigned from the *New Masses.* As he said in the letter that Mike Gold printed under a banner headline, he had wished to be associated with the magazine at first "because it represented a partly Communist and at any rate rebellious literary tendency" with which he sympathized. But he now thought the publication seemed "chiefly to represent . . . a neurotic literary and pictorial aestheticism" which he did not like at all. "Yours for the Revolution," he said at the end.[20] As Daniel Aaron writes, "Gold now spit on his hands, rolled up his sleeves, and wrote a merciless denunciation of his old associate and 'apostate' radical."[21] Gold's letter is filled with accusations: Dell is a psychoanalyst, a Village playboy, a sex racketeer, a cheap literary careerist; his writings are but confessions of his own love life and marriage. Indeed, Dell, Gold concludes, is really dead; and, by rights, he should not have signed his letter as a revolutionist.

Gold was partly right. Dell had not been, as both of them well knew, a revolutionist in the Marxian—and Goldian—sense of the word; nor had Dell practiced novel-writing or criticism as Gold—or any person or dogma—would dictate. In their decade of contention, Gold surely knew that Dell's social heritage flowed from such writers as Ruskin, Carlyle, Emerson, Whitman, Ingersoll, rather than from Marx or Lenin. And there were other differences between them: Dell's heritage had been rural, grass-roots; Gold's, urban. For all his sophistication, Dell had come from the Midwest, from small towns; success had come quickly and, for all his work and early poverty, rather easily. Gold, a Jew from the East Side slums of New York, with a different heritage and upbringing, believed in action and violence; and he believed that art and propaganda could assist that action.

The truth is that Dell had a double attitude toward politics and art. Politics was one thing; art, something else. "I was always," he wrote in a letter in 1964, "in some respect a Socialist, one who wanted to change the world, and in sympathy with the workers in their revolt against oppression." As for politics and art, he agreed with Shaw: "What we want is not music for the people, but bread for the people, rest for the people, immunity from robbery and scorn for the people, hope for them, enjoyment, equal respect and consideration, life and aspiration, instead of drudgery and despair. When we get that I imagine the people will make tolerable music for themselves, even if all Beethoven's scores perish in the interim."

Dell then asserts: "I always felt that way (and I still do). I also have interests that are non-political, which I do not (and never did) confuse with the others. . . ." Some writers are interested in "self-expression and not at all in world-improvement"; some, like Upton Sinclair, "confuse the two." "I have never," he writes, "supposed that politics, revolutionary or other, was a sufficient foundation for literature or any of the other arts. As a novelist I wrote from a different point of view than I did as a Socialist journalist."[22] Indeed, like the other editors of *The Masses,* Dell had worked and thought as a Socialist, not as an artist or an art propagandist. As he wrote in 1947: "as for me, I belonged to the neo-Aristotelian school of aesthetics which holds that 'certainly the world should be reformed: but not by novels.' "[23]

In resigning, then, from a magazine that proposed to do one thing but seemed to be doing another, Dell was following a line of reasonable consistency. As he writes, "When I quit the *New Masses* it was because that magazine had become very arty in

the modernistic ways of those times and because its editors supposed that this was 'revolutionary'—and it wasn't political and
Socialist enough to suit me. . . ."[24] Although he had written
about social misery and despair, about a culture that often
stifled and shackled freedom, he wrote as a novelist mainly of
the individual's inner life, the growth, the change, the adjustment to a world of work and love, the pursuit and sometimes
the discovery of a fine ideal. Even so, Dell was neither the militant organizer nor the strike leader. His was the recording voice
that believed and said that he believed—and said so in charming
and graceful, although sometimes petulant prose. Perhaps he
was speaking of the dual aspects of his own life when he wrote
in *Love in Greenwich Village*: "Whoever has once lived for unreal things, such as without any disrespect one may call Beauty
or Truth or the Future, can never in an utterly simple way be at
home among life's realities, however good and innocent these
realities may be. He can only try to—and remain an alien" (319).

CHAPTER 7

Dell as Novelist in the Late 1920's

DELL HAD spent the end of 1925 and the early part of 1926 preparing *Intellectual Vagabondage* and *Love in Greenwich Village* for publication, but by autumn he had his new novel, *An Old Man's Folly,* ready for his publishers. Careless and carefree as he and his ideas may have seemed to many, he continued to write with the integrity and learning of the professional man of letters. Surely the many years of writing and editing, of meeting deadlines and making decisions, had encouraged a discipline that had become—or always was—integral to his personality. *An Old Man's Folly* became his fifth novel—the eleventh volume—in six years; and, before the decade ended, in addition to the little pamphlet on *The Outline of Marriage* in 1926-27 and the edition of *The Anatomy of Melancholy* with Paul Jordan-Smith in 1927, Dell had published *An Unmarried Father* in 1927; converted it with the help of Thomas Mitchell into a successful Broadway play in 1928; and in 1929, written the final volume to the Felix Fay trilogy. As both critic and novelist, he continued to be a writer of great productivity; and his was one of the leading voices against the stifling effects of the old genteel tradition, which many writers of the last three decades, and especially the 1920's, had reacted so strongly against. But now there were new considerations.

By the mid-1920's, fiction had already greatly changed in the direction that Dell had hoped it would take. Since the Chicago days, he had assailed, like many others, the sentimental, tame, conventional, even dull standards of the genteel monthly magazines. He had wished for a sane and sensible acceptance of life as it was being lived; he had wished for frankness—especially about sex—and now frankness was there. But there was also something else, and in his essay "Critic's Magic," in 1926, he summarizes his critical attitude and beliefs with candor: "I could not guess how much of coprophilic dirt handling, of sadistic sexual hatred and cruelty, of mawkish homosexual disgust of life, was to be unveiled and paraded in the frank new literature which was to come into existence according to my wish!"[1] Dell had "thought of sexual frankness in normal and happy terms—a noble nudity was what I looked for"; and he found the constant "elucidation of abnormal types" mostly a bore. If he wanted instruction on such themes, he preferred to read scientific literature with its "steadfast judgment of these aberrations in the light of normality. . . ."[2]

In addition to frankness, Dell believed that fiction ought to be serious, not neurotic. Neurotic fiction is "concerned with oversensitive persons, to whom the kind of life which other people go through cheerfully and easily enough is a torment, a bewilderment, a misery, a burden too grievous to be borne."[3] Popular in the wake of World War I, neurotic fiction, he continues, gave people whose beliefs were shattered a "false dignity to their feeling of helplessness."[4] Actually, says Dell, such writers have but lost "their grip on reality." Their pictures of life are but distortions that "make life seem more terrible than it is."[5]

And he had another objection to the new fiction—the language. Impatient with old standards, he saw that "even the standard of ordinary literate English" had been smashed. Even if diction fell to the "level of the document," "it is not too much," he believed, "to ask that a writer should also be able to write."[6]

Although critical of new developments in literature, Dell has not so much changed his standards and attitudes as redefined them. Novelists always had to ask two essential questions: ". . . what sort of lives are most worth living, and are we missing anything we ought to be getting?"[7] The function of the novelist was to discover the new America of the machine age. Although such discoveries had been made earlier in the century, they were little more than "a description and interpretation and dramatization of what was found to be characteristic of America."[8] Then, as writers began to deal with the forces of human nature, moral and political interpretations gave way to economic and psychological conceptions; and, in an effort to understand these forces, writers sometimes substituted neurotic mysticism for intellectual approaches and began to interpret life by a "vaguely mystical and superstitious worship of the Great Forces of Nature. . . ."[9] The sense of reality in fiction may, of course, be approached through mysticism, as in the writings of Sherwood Anderson, or through scientific knowledge, as in the writings of Glasgow, Lewis, or Charles Norris. Dell thought the last three better able to answer essential questions, for he wished writers "to have the scientific basis, to know their economics and their psychology, . . . to face life without fear, and to proceed gallantly with the literary discovery of America! . . ."[10]

Ironically, Dell's prescription for the writer makes way for the very kind of limitless experimentation that he criticized. What is truth to him is to another only the dogma that needs be overthrown. Long before his break with the *New Masses* and his rejection of "neurotic literary and pictorial aestheticism," a younger generation had criticized him. As he had written in 1923: "The generations move swiftly in these days, and I, who am still a member of a younger generation which had just begun to get a foothold in the citadel of public taste, find myself denounced by a still younger generation as one of that gang of tyrants and oppressors whose authority must be destroyed if literature in America is ever to come into its own."[11]

In *Homecoming,* Dell recalls how Waldo Frank had once told him that he expected him to write in the "experimental modern way, and not in the old, formal Victorian way. . . ." Dell had replied, "By the time you have triumphantly demonstrated the virtues of the new way of writing novels, I hope to have learned the old-fashioned way of writing them."[12] Whatever the inconsistency attributed to him, Dell was consistent in his practice of and demands for the novel; and, in showing how the folly of a man may lead also to his salvation, he attempts once more to come to grips with the questions: what sort of life is worth living? Are we missing anything we ought to be getting? *An Old Man's Folly,* which he later called a "romantic novel," was published in October, 1926.

I   An Old Man's Folly

An Old Man's Folly is not a bedroom romance or a family novel of middle-class life, as accusations would have it, although the growth of a family and the importance of love are part of the complex picture that Dell describes. Instead, the story is about an outsider, an alien living mostly alone, but with a wife and family and in a society and a business that he has made a career. A man of dreams and ideals, his pursuit of folly leads not to ruin and defeat, as the world proclaims it will, but to self-fulfillment and to happiness. A variation on the theme of the mad ideal, *An Old Man's Folly* is the story of Nathaniel Windle, who not only seeks refuge "from a world which he did not like and into which he didn't fit" (100), but who also discovers both a new world of meaning and a new meaning and identity in himself. Since the new world that Windle discovers and the old world from which he alienates himself involve both old and new generations, as well as old and new ideas, the novel describes a clash of attitudes at a point in time: the hero's radical activities are set within the historical framework of the pacifist movement of World War I.

In *Runaway* Dell had plotted the novel in chapters with titles reminiscent of Fielding. In *An Old Man's Folly* he divides his story into three books and begins the history of the hero in the 1850's. His portrayal of the growth of an individual against the shifting scenes of public events and social issues enables him to merge the personal and historical and to show how the passage of time and events weave the pattern of an era. Nowhere else has Dell examined with greater competency the psychological problem of an individual whose rebellion has alienated him from the world about him, but whose aim is to belong to and be accepted by at least a part of that world. An elderly vagabond, the hero is "quickened into new life by contact with a more or less revolutionary boy and girl."

Not unlike other Dell heroes, Nathaniel Windle's life has been that of the double man. While his father has scoffed at his mother's idealism and tried to direct his son into the sensible world of business, the boy, very much alone, has grown up with a fear of the "ideal" and a dislike of "real." As he reads from Emerson's *Essays* to his dying mother and worships his cousin Christopher, whose adventures in the artistic world are a reality that his father will not admit, the boy becomes more uncertain of himself. Since "this Outside realm" of imaginative exploration seems but "chaos," his timidity makes him prefer "the certainty and safety of the familiar and the expected"—the business world (18). The death of his mother and of Christopher, and then of his father, shapes the separation of the world of dreams and actual life: the two hundred dollars that comes to him as a result of Christopher's death and the letter telling him to squander the money on "something beautiful and foolish," are put into the volume of Emerson's essays and laid aside for forty-nine years. With this symbolic burial of his dreams and ideals, he becomes a successful salesman of bustles. Tyrannized by fear, yet "ruled by a desperate pride," young Windle is left with "an anxiety" over the failure that he feels himself to be.

Living the masquerade of a sensible man for the next half century, Windle commits two clearly irrational acts during that time. At the very beginning, he impulsively asks another man's fiancée to go for a walk with him; and, while the two are really very happy together, he does not marry Ada, who does not marry anyone. Windle, returning to Mabel Spang, marries "the wrong girl just because he had promised to. . ." (50), and he settles down with his petty and ambitious wife, and in time, their only daughter.

Although he catches glimpses of events passing him by from his occasional refuge in the corner saloon or as a traveling corset salesman, Windle is fifty years old before destiny plays a real joke on him. His uncle in California dies, leaving him a half-interest in a wallpaper business; and the Windles move to California to become partners in a business that they know nothing about. After a decade, Windle gives up to his business-minded son-in-law, and retires. A witness one evening to the break-up of a workers' demonstration, he commits the "second irrational and impulsive act" of his life (101): he mounts a soapbox to speak. Before he can utter a word, he is arrested and taken to jail. Betrayed, as it were, by the "treacherous part of his mind," he has, like some modern Robinson Crusoe, become a "shipwreck on a strange coast." But, regarded as a fellow Socialist by the little group of radicals, he finds himself, as Dell says, entering a "new world."

To enter the "new world" on the night of the Red Dawn ball, as Windle sees and as the name suggests," is to become aware of a new day, of the "sensual beauty and happiness" that "American material progress and conquest of leisure" have brought in those years before the war. And he likes the Peace Society, where he feels spiritually at home, as well as the odd assortment of teachers, newsmen, Socialists, intellectuals, each a little lonely, but filled with youthful fervor, who make up the group. He sees that they are "implicitly united by their common differences," and he believes that they are asking sensible questions: what sort of life is worth living? How can one help oneself? How can one help others?

In a sense their questions have always been his questions, and Windle's discovery of his new world is not unlike his earlier discovery of Emerson's essays: his use of the past, his awareness of the present, his commitment to action have made Windle a seer and shaper of the lives of others. His experience at the Red Dawn ball takes him back into his past; the dance floor, alive with rebellious youth, reminds him of his cousin Christopher, the "afternoon with Ada," and of his meeting with the radicals —of those two impulsive acts that have finally led him to an awareness of the real world of 1916 and to the discovery that he belongs to and is accepted by the young radicals. Belonging makes him aware of losses; and part of his function in the story is to mirror that awareness, to become a kind of sounding board of sensibilities like the character in a Henry James novel, but the reference to James is merely implicit, although one of the characters in *An Old Man's Folly* is rereading James's works. Thus, Windle becomes both the instructed and the enlightened one; and, if he sees the "new world" as fantasy, as he actually does on the night of the Red Dawn ball, his seeing springs from the kind of wraithlike shape that he has actually been throughout the novel. Now his vision and his "self" are one, and what makes his presence significant is both his capability of committing what people in the business world call an "irrational folly," and his inspiriting influence on his radical friends who are intent on reshaping world events. Not only has Windle become a kind of Emersonian seer, but he has also shared that vision with others.

Actually, Windle's vision of the future—that "promise of something more, something still to come," the "recurrent dream" in which he is young again and walks with a golden-haired sweetheart (135)—remains unfulfilled and unrealized until he meets Ann Elizabeth Landor, a young college girl who is interested in social causes and is partly modeled on Dell's second wife; and Joe Ford, the young married reporter on the *News-Chronicle,* who has witnessed Windle's arrest. In identifying Joe and Ann Elizabeth with Christopher and Ada, Windle sees his new friends as the visible counterpart of what his own life might have been. Although he can only "look on," he feels, like John Marcher in James's "The Beast in the Jungle," as if "something very wonderful and exciting was waiting for me around the next corner" (147-48). To convert his dream into reality, Windle needs a guide to help him distinguish fact from fancy.

As a high-school teacher of English who has devoted herself to observing others and is now rereading Henry James, Susan Beaver, perhaps more than any other character in the novel, best serves as Windle's guide. Agent as well as agency, a teacher of life in general, she questions and describes, collects data and files it, arranges events, and brings people together. Psychologist and confessor, she wonders what little "forgotten incident" may have changed people's lives "from conformity to rebellion" (140); for she believes that rebellion comes, not only from intellectual convictions, but from "some crisis" in man's life. She seeks that moment of change, that point of decision from which comes a new course of action.

Susan's role is both to direct people's lives and to help people reveal their personalities. She finds that behind the near ruthless propagandizing of Ann Elizabeth Landor lies the story of a father whose own youthful rebellion had turned into intense hatred for everything German. She learns, too, that Mr. Windle's secret dream of uniting Ann Elizabeth and Joe Ford in marriage is a way of recapturing "his lost youth, his unfulfilled wishes"; and Susan senses that the explosive force which has impelled him into his new world now makes him count on "such a thing happening in real earnest." If Mr. Windle somehow sits in the middle and "knows," Susan Beaver brings that knowledge to the surface.

As an enlightened seer and truth-seeker, Windle actually has become a destructive, disruptive force. The little personal quarrels in the "peace" society seem not unrelated to those larger public quarrels which are destroying and changing old patterns. The love affair of Ann Elizabeth with Dave Bursley, whose opinions are "invariably like those of the respectable mob" (199), begins to dissolve with arguments over the Russian Revolution. The marriage of Joe Ford to a wife who is committed "to respectability, to ambition, to regularity, to success, to ordinariness" (184), receives its fatal blow when Ford refuses to attack the radical minister, Dr. Starkweather, who has been arrested and charged with disturbing the peace. The new world toward which Windle and Ann Elizabeth and now Joe Ford gravitate is hardly a safe refuge from past or future. Actually this New Atlantis leads each individual into a kind of "rebel province of that meaningless and cruel world outside" that "seemed beleaguered now by overwhelming forces" (245).

Thus, as the personal problems of the characters become entwined with public issues, *An Old Man's Folly* reads as social history. Dell makes integral to the personal lives of his characters the devastating effects of the high emotionalism that accompanied World War I:

Every day reports came in of meetings being raided, of people beaten up, arrested, sent to prison. The Espionage Act had been passed, and twenty-year sentences were being given to war-dissidents. Not to buy Liberty Bonds meant losing one's job, or being called before a self-constituted local Vigilance Committee and accused of treasonable views, with a stenographer taking notes to be laid before the next Grand Jury. It seemed, from any practical point of view, useless to resist the efficient terrorism with which all protest against the war was being silenced throughout America. (246)

Many other issues of the war era appear in the novel: the election of President Wilson, the role and rights of conscientious objectors; the economics of war; the arrest and imprisonment of ministers like Dr. Starkweather; the breakdown of family relationships; the destruction of nations, of the Peace Society; and finally the trial under the Espionage Act of those who dared resist for whatever honorable and worthy reasons. Involved as Dell had been in the social history of his own time, he has clearly utilized autobiographical incidents as well as public events. Like his characters, he has been both observer and participant; in describing such actions as the police raid on the offices of the Peace Society, he writes with a dramatic swiftness that maintains the balance between the impersonal sway of events and personal involvement.

In Book Three, which Dell calls "The Legacy," the answer to the question of what sort of life is worth living comes in terms of New York, not California. Mr. Windle returns from Europe, and Joe Ford is released from prison; they both meet Ann Elizabeth in Greenwich Village, where she has been working on a liberal weekly. Landing in New York in that month of March when President Wilson is speaking of the League of Nations at the Metropolitan Opera House and militant suffragettes are picketing the place, Mr. Windle escapes from his hotel with the old cigarbox under his arm and goes to the Village to indulge his last folly: to Joe Ford he gives the two-hundred-dollar legacy, which all these years has been acquiring meaning but no interest between the pages of Emerson's essays. Together they seek Ann Elizabeth, whose parading with the suffragettes is an episode reminiscent of a similar one that involved Dell and B. Marie. Although Windle dies a few weeks later as a result of the escapade, he has already achieved a synthesis of dream and reality, of rebellion and acquiescence to life. After such defiance, what forgiveness? After such rebellion and destruction, what kind of life is worthy?

Dell answers such questions in terms of the artist, just as he had in real life. By the early 1920's Joe Ford has an editorial job in New York. He commutes daily from their little house in Jersey (as Dell had once done), where he and Ann Elizabeth live a rather poor but vital life with their two children. His novel has been put aside for the mere business of making a living. As Susan Beaver observes, there is a contentment about them; they talk of art, jazz, and African masks; they use the language of psychoanalysis; they discuss Russia with a "non-political slant." Have they become conservative? "Not in our ideas perhaps, but certainly in our habits," says Ann Elizabeth (361). Less earnest, more inclined to play than in the old days, they are perhaps "lucky enough to have found in this troubled world even a commonplace happiness" (352). But they are creating, not destroying. In living what turns out to be "really an old-fashioned kind of life" (361), they have achieved a legacy of more than money: they have discovered the happiness of living in accordance with their own dreams and desires. An old man's folly becomes, therefore, their inherited wisdom.

II   An Unmarried Father

In *An Old Man's Folly,* Dell had been concerned with a number of social issues. In *An Unmarried Father,* published on the last day of September, 1927, he was not, as he has said, intentionally "concerned with larger sociological problems" at all, but with how it would "feel to find myself in that situation— which I made less acutely personal by making my young man somewhat like my friend Arthur Ficke, socially."[13] But in the clash with conventional morality, partly revealed through the hero's relation with his father and with his own son, the novel becomes, in part, an ironic protest against the neurotic attitudes and values of society toward sex in general and toward illegitimacy in particular.

An Unmarried Father is neither moving nor profound. With the novel's single plot movement, its clear-cut presentation of character, and its uncomplicated development of character relationships, it tells the story of an amusing and romantic incident; and, if pretentious and implausible, it toys with serious considerations and offers sensible and scientific comment along with the sermons and statistics. It merits consideration, partly as contrast to Dell's other novels, and partly because of its success, not so much as a novel, but as a Broadway play and as a Hollywood movie.

Yet, the problem that Dell explores in *An Unmarried Father* is serious: what happens to a child fathered out of wedlock when the mother refuses it, but the father does not? What can be done to help illegitimate children achieve a personally satisfactory role in a society that places a stigma on their birth? In reversing the usual situation by making the father more responsible to the child than the mother, Dell has given a new twist to an old but continuing dilemma.

The story of *An Unmarried Father* begins with a realistic and dramatic event: the hero, Norman Overbeck, a young lawyer of apparently conventional and proper morals, receives a letter from an adoption society in Chicago, asking that he come at once on a personal matter. Overbeck has become the father of an illegitimate baby boy; and, while the problem is personal, Dell's psychological study of a modern love affair has its ancient parallel, as the name of the patron saint of the Saint Thecla Child Adoption Society suggests, in the story of Thecla and Paul of Thamyris and Alexander, found in the Acts of Paul in the Apocrypha of the New Testament.

Thecla, a young Iconian girl, betrothed to Thamyris, becomes

enamoured of the discourses of Paul. Refusing to marry her
suitor, Thecla follows Paul to Antioch; and there a magistrate,
Alexander, falls in love with her, although she protests his interest. Dell ends the parallel at this point, but clearly the hero—
Norman Overbeck, a young lawyer—is Alexander; Isabel Drury,
the girl he has met at College, is Thecla. And Thecla's love for
the Gospel of Paul is Isabel's love for modern art, but it may also be Dr. Zerneke's love for the adoption society, or Mrs.
Czermak's love and need for children, and partly Norman's and
Isabel's belief in the gospel of love themselves. This devotion to
an idea that reflects Thecla's own love of the gospel is exhibited
by several characters; and, while Dell clarifies his use of the anal-
ogy toward the end of the novel, he has made it integral to the
meaning, if not the structure of the story, from the beginning.

Divided into three books, the novel begins in Vickley, the fictional Mississippi town of the Felix Fay story, with the discovery
of the hero's illegitimate son and Isabel's devotion to art; develops with the hero's "exile" in Chicago, where he rescues his
own son and takes care of him; and ends with the "dominant
sex"—and the hero—returning to the seemingly conventional
settlement of marriage and forgiveness.

In view of Dell's own anticonventional ideas, his choice of a
hero with fairly conventional views and attitudes seems hardly
consistent with his liberal past, especially since he neither rejects
the hero nor holds him up to satiric ridicule. Norman Overbeck's
love affair at Cambridge with an art student seems at first glance
only a masculine deviation that is part of conventional predict-
ability. Even his name seems a pun on the normal life that he
leads. Engaged to a local Vickley girl, Madge Ferris, he still lives
with his family, while his father's domination of his two daugh-
ters and one son makes him a tyrant of conventional stamp. But
the letter from Dr. Zerneke that asks young Overbeck to come
to Chicago to sign papers for his own child's adoption prompts
a response not unlike that of Thecla. He rebels against an older
generation and, at the same time, discovers that, as with his own
behavior, conventional thinking is often given to doing one
thing in public and another in private. When he learns that
Isabel wants to pursue a career in art rather than marry, he does
a rather unconventional thing: he tells his fiancée about the
child; leaves Vickley, goes to Chicago, finds a job; and proposes

to take care of the baby himself. He discovers, of course, that a man has—and Dell's point is that he perhaps should—as much trouble with the problem of illegitimacy as do women. The agency is willing that his family take the child, but it regards him as incapable and irresponsible as a parent.

What Norman Overbeck seeks is a sensible and personally satisfactory answer to what is, of course, an absurd and rare problem. Being sensible with others and with himself is not easy. Conventions have so befogged the issue that, while society acknowledges—even accepts—the child, it constantly does so for wrong reasons, for romantic and exotic reasons. Gilbert Rand, lawyer friend from Vickley, who serves as both adviser and messenger to the inner thoughts of the home-town citizenry, convinces those "hard-boiled reprobates at Sam's bar" that most men really pride themselves on sexual prowess; that Vickley matrons look on a young man who tries to expiate "his youthful sin by self-sacrifice" as romantic and wonderful; that even a fiancée, secretly rebelling herself, accepts the child with dignity and respect; that even Norman's father has had a clandestine affair—as if what has happened to Norman is but part of human history that no convention can erase. Is the tribe then so terrible after all? The truth is that a home and parents are needed for the child's welfare; bachelor's quarters, an institution, or a jobless father will not serve as a substitute. As Dr. Zerneke sees, the problem is answered not by romantic acceptance of the consequences of "tribal error" but by the business of taking care of the child, finding it a mother, and getting on with the business of sane living.

In Book Three, "The Dominant Sex," Dell criticizes conventional male arrogance and presents his views on the need for reexamining the laws of legitimation. As if speaking from experience, he sees that any love affair may have human implications that mere talk can not expiate. He allows his hero to see that a mother, a sister, and a fiancée are of necessity involved in the relationships; that his little affair with Monica Case, whatever the human inclinations of the male, attests the neurotic and romantic idealism of the conventional rebel. As a lawyer, young Overbeck checks on the more liberal approach to legitimation in Norway, Sweden, and Russia; but he questions whether legal procedures—like talk and rationalization—have outwitted the vagaries of human nature. Although property rights may often take precedence over human rights, the family, Dell clearly implies, has an integrity that legality can neither provide nor destroy.

What, then, is the sensible solution to a serious social and personal dilemma? While marriage to either Madge or Monica will satisfy the demands of society, marriage to neither will solve the hero's feelings of loss and despair. As he rereads the story of Thecla, he realizes that his own life of conventional attitudes has all but obscured his affection and respect for that person who devoted herself to an ideal. As he gains a measure of self-insight, he feels compassion for Isabel, even forgiveness, as if he "had put aside his youth for ever" (295). His return to Isabel is inevitable. *An Unmarried Father* is a lighthearted and humorous attack on society's conventional and neurotic attitudes toward illegitimacy, but it is a serious statement about man's and woman's responsibility to each other in such a dilemma.

III   *Broadway Playwright*

Whether or not Dell had originally thought of turning *An Unmarried Father* into the play he called *Little Accident*, he surely saw the dramatic qualities of the novel. As he recalls in a newspaper story of the time: "I sat down and wrote the first draft of 'Little Accident' all by myself." Crosby Gaige, who finally presented the play, saw possibilities in the nine scenes that Dell had devised and introduced him to Thomas Mitchell, a young actor and playwright, who rewrote the scenes into three acts and added several characters. Like the novel, the play reverses the usual sentiments: the mother is less interested in the child than in the art career in Paris; the father is bent on sacrificing his career in law for the sake of keeping the child. Although the second and third acts were rewritten several times, the three acts were built around three events: Norman Overbeck's receiving of the letter that informs him that he is father of a baby boy; the episode in the reception room of the maternity hospital in Chicago; and finally the episode in the boardinghouse where the hero has taken his own kidnapped child, and where the child's mother finally comes, having given up art for marriage and family.

Dell himself helped with casting the play, and sat in on rehearsals. But, as he says, the final play is also Mitchell's. Mitchell had apparently changed Dell's "long and very Shavian" speeches into conversation and had insisted on omitting statistics on illegitimacy and legal explanations. Dell wrote that Mitchell had turned "a sociological anecdote that was funny because it couldn't help being into a delightful Irish fairy tale."[14]

Opening October 9, 1928, at the Morosco Theatre in New York with Thomas Mitchell as the unwed father, Katherine Alexander as the husbandless mother of the child, and Elvia Enders as the fiancée, *Little Accident* ran for 289 performances and proved to be one of the eight or ten successful plays of the 1928-29 season. While Dell had never made much money from his novels, *Little Accident* brought him from one hundred to five hundred dollars a week for a while. The reviewers found the play delightfully amusing, perhaps the "season's most entertaining comedy." George Jean Nathan, hard to please at best, said that, although "it got under way very slowly," it gave "interest and pleasure." *Little Accident* received the 1929 Megrue Prize for comedy.

Dell's first Broadway play had succeeded as theater; but, like the novel from which it was taken, *Little Accident* was not highly regarded by some critics: it was assailed by both the radical Left and the religious Right. R. Dana Skinner, writing in *The Commonweal,* found that "in its utter falsity to the realities of life, so far as its main theme goes, it turns all values topsy-turvy." His criticism of the specific play takes on a general note: "If there is any one thing from which modern life is suffering—and tragically, too—it is failure to see life through, to understand the interaction of events, the tragedy which may spring from carelessness and unbridled egoism, and the responsibility which goes with every human act."[15]

However, the play had additional successes. Sold to Universal Pictures, it appeared as one of the early sound films in the summer of 1930, starring Douglas Fairbanks, Jr., as Norman Overbeck and Anita Page as Isabel Drury. In 1944 the story was remade as *Casanova Brown* with Gary Cooper, Teresa Wright, and Frank Morgan. In this new version written by Nunnally Johnson, the whole affair takes on an air of legitimacy: although once married, the couple is separated. Some of the fun remains.

Dell collaborated with Mitchell again in 1931 on a new play,

Cloudy with Showers, the story of an English professor and an escapade with one of his women students; but the effort proved less successful with a Broadway run of seventy-one performances.

IV   *Dell's Achievement*

With the publication of *Souvenir* in 1929, already discussed in Chapter 4, and with work well under way on his long study of love and adaptation in the machine world, Dell continued to contribute to the world of letters and in a variety of fields. Not yet forty-five years old, he had already been a leader in two important—perhaps three—literary circles: one in Chicago, and two in New York, if a distinction is made between the Greenwich Village before World War I and the one after. As Emily Hahn has recently said, "Few know as much about the eastward drift of the artist as the writer Floyd Dell, who went through it all and might well claim to be a textbook case."[16] In 1930, *The Bookman,* edited by Seward Collins, commented on Dell's significance:

In fact Dell has probably embraced in his career more of the elements that went to make up the 'twenties than any other person. Merely to list them telegraphically is to sum up the whole era: Illinois village—Iowa town—Chicago journalism—newspaper book-reviewing—socialism—feminism—Greenwich Village—psycho-analysis—pacificism—Greenwich Village theatricals—Greenwich Village radicalism—Greenwich Village amour—autobiographical novel—more autobiography—suppression by censors. He even ends the decade in the representative fashion, with a waning fame and an obvious inclination to suspect that the red-hot doctrines of the past twenty years were not after all the ultimate truths.[17]

When the crash in 1929 brought an end to the "jazz age" and the beginning of the depression of the 1930's, Dell was not, perhaps, as astounded at a world of threadbare economy as were many of his younger contemporaries. As a poor boy from the Midwest who had personally known poverty and struggle, he already knew how economic deprivation could warp dreams and destroy ideals. Like Huck Finn, he "had been there before."

CHAPTER 8

Dell in the 1930's

IF FLOYD DELL suspected that his fame was waning in 1930, as *The Bookman* said, and that his doctrines were not ultimate truths, he neither became silent nor found new directions for his thinking. Living still in Croton-on-Hudson, where he had resided during the 1920's, he was, if anything, happier, more independent, and in 1929, more successful financially than he had ever been. He had just written a popular Broadway play that soon became a successful movie; as a lecturer, he was sought after and well received.

When the economic crash came in 1929, Dell had already resigned from the *New Masses.* Still sympathetic to socialism and revolutionary doctrine, he had no public or official connection with the new proletarian writers of the political Left. He had not given up his interest in political and social problems, nor had he changed his thinking on most subjects from the Chicago and New York days. He had, of course, given up the practice of free love; he was now happily married. But on social and political issues, he remained the revolutionary liberal who had been writing about such problems for the past twenty years. In a sense, he had started from the revolutionary and radical point of view that many new writers were now adopting in politics and—as he had not done—in art. Although his life was to take a new direction in the mid-1930's as a result of the depression, Dell's success in marriage and as a novelist had up to 1930 made 1919 and 1920 far more significant dates in his life than 1929.

The success of Dell's first novel and his continuing success as an independent writer had given his relation to the world a new dimension. As book reviewer, editor, and journalist, he had worked closely with men who were helping to shape the contemporary world. Although he lingered for a time in the Village, made a number of lecture tours, and continued to write essays, articles, and reviews, his life as a novelist was that of a man working alone: he was still the outsider, the observer, the artist reflecting; and, while contemporary elements creep into his work, much of his writing during the 1920's is a matter of memory and imagination, the reflections on a bygone era, the remembrance of life already lived. Often, of course, the past that figures in the novels may be presented as conventional attitudes and narrow social views; and these are rejected and rebelled against, sometimes by both young and old. But the rebellion is more an individual revolt than a planned social action; and, although the novels contain both direct and implied social criticism, they are neither programs nor prescriptions for changing the world. Rather, Dell continues to examine human problems and motives, to explore individual reactions, habits, customs, and ideals. As novelist, he is neither propagandist nor reformer.

With the 1930's and with many writers choosing the side of the workers, as Malcolm Cowley once said they should, Dell keeps to his own vision of truth. There may be an acceleration in his publications, but his thinking has the same independence and integrity of belief that always characterized it. After his acceptance of a government position in 1935, he has less time for writing; but his record of publication during the first four years of the 1930's is impressive: a psychological study of love in the modern world, three novels, the autobiography up to 1923, a pamphlet on education, and the Broadway play (with Thomas Mitchell) in 1931. His energies and abilities seem without end or dimunition. If he suffered waning fame, his powers were not waning—either mentally or physically.

I   Love in the Machine Age

In *Were You Ever a Child?* and *The Outline of Marriage*—as well as in countless articles, the novels, short stories, poetry, plays—Dell had already written about love and marriage and education; but his long study in these areas, *Love in the Machine Age, a Psychological Study of the Transition from Patriarchal Society* (1930), is the solid and impressive synthesis and statement of his many years of thinking about the complex and perplexing problems of what it is like to grow up in a rapidly

changing technological world and to live in it as a sanely orient-
ed adult. Although *Love in the Machine Age* is calculated to
help people change their lives, it is no manifesto for program-
matic social change: it is a well-researched and well-documented
study of individual and social behavior in both the past and the
present.

Love in the Machine Age is a historical, biological, and psychological account "of a middle-class revolution," a commitment to "revolutionary social views," but not "to any specific
revolutionary procedure" (201). Restating recent psychology
"as far as possible in sociological and historical terms" (5), and
using the techniques of case worker and scientist, Dell aims "to
popularize a modern and scientific view of behavior, and there-
by to help people to live happy and successful lives" (3). Working against a "historical background," he discusses the problems
of modern life—of love, marriage, children, education, work, economics; the function of knowledge; the importance of individual emotional happiness; the need for enjoying "responsible
social and economic relations to others" (3).

Man's problem, as Dell sees it, is to adjust himself to the new
world of the machine in which he perforce must live; and he
must begin by casting off the relics and traditions of the "patriarchal regime" of the Middle Ages and accept new ways of seeing and believing. At first those new ways may seem like sheer
anarchy, but such a break is necessary if man is to achieve his
freedom and happiness. Compromises, especially "patriarchal
sex-compromises," have no place in the modern world (8). Although Dell makes use of verifiable evidence, his argument begins with an assertion and develops toward a conceptual ideal.

Much of man's difficulty, Dell writes, lies with the fact that
the normal biological instincts have been thwarted by the economic and social beliefs and by customs of a patriarchal society.
The normal pattern develops through two stages: from infancy
to puberty, when the child learns to "love others beside himself"; and from puberty onward, when glandular changes "normally complete this process of psychic development" (15).
"Normal" development includes the activities of flirtation, love
choice, sexual mating, parenthood, and family life, with the
"deepest love-interests" centering psychologically "in persons

of the other sex"; and finally a "capacity for sustained efforts to gain food and shelter" comes "with an increase in size and muscular strength" (15). But in a patriarchal society, which is sustained by ruling castes; by slavery, serfdom, landed property, prostitution; and by the military, the patriarchal family and system can seldom honor individual talents or careers, creative impulses, and choices in love and work. Normal instinctive processes thus become frustrated, and sexual impulses are often redirected into illicit relations with girls and boys of the lower classes or with slaves, in arranged marriages and adultery, in homosexual practices, in prostitution and bastardy, or in sacred celibacy within the church.

Finally, when the middle class began breaking the pattern, it tended more to imitate than to rebel. Consequently, man's need of learning about himself and about love, of freely choosing a mate, of considering men and women as social equals, and of encouraging an instinctive family and parental life of a genuine and lasting kind remained an impossible achievement. Divorce has helped as a way of partly correcting errors, but it is no solution to the ideal of a lifelong marriage based on love and affection.

Although the introduction of modern machinery has given men and women the opportunity of making their own choices in love and work, there are still difficulties. Many educational methods, for example, still foster patriarchal attitudes. Children are taught to respect their elders; and many young men and women, the victims of parental fixation, end up being truer to their mothers and fathers than to their wives and husbands. Sometimes, during the economic shocks of sudden prosperity and lack of employment, children, who have been trained to depend on authority, become pimps or members of a gang. In many cases, parents themselves, primarily concerned with preserving their own private universes, have little real wisdom to offer their children, whether it be old-fashioned conventions or "advanced thinking."

Although the family may try to retain its privilege of being wise in all fields including dress and manner, the child receives a greater directive influence from the outside, from schools and colleges. As Dell says, "each generation knows what constitutes attractiveness for its members, and will fight to achieve it. Only the wholesomely meek will follow obsolete patterns" (107). The way out, Dell writes, is to allow each person "to choose for himself, according to his own needs, what guidance he will follow" (112). Without the ability, training, or hope to make free choices, a child remains frustrated, eternally adolescent: ". . . *our stability,"* writes Dell, *"must be in our possession of powers of choice"* (115).

But Dell is clearly aware that in a world of rapid change, where conventions have been shattered and confusion is the order of the day, boys and girls will have a hard time making choices and in threading their way through the period of adolescence. In consequence, they may take several paths in dealing with their mental conflicts: they may resort to a double personality so that lapses in control may be quickly forgotten or denied by another self; they may project their faults on others and withdraw into the "caves of dream"; they may identify themselves with neurotic suffering in the outside world; they may even find a path of knowledge to psychic health that corrects the relations between the past and themselves.

Furthermore, in a transitional time when mankind is "reluctant to adapt its way of thinking to changed economic conditions," attempts at adjustment often become compromises or turn out simply to be old ideas in disguise. What Dell calls "ideological overcompensations" have, he believes, done more to detach people from the past than to afford visions of the future (117). For example, state nurseries that have tried to replace the family in rehabilitating the child have generally failed. More freedom in sex has been granted, but sex seen merely as amusement is but the continuation of the patriarchal sex-compromise; no solution, it is only an evasion. More women are working, but for them to make work and a career their only goal is "strictly a middle-class overcompensation against parasitism." Since, according to Dell, work is the means and "the end is love, marriage, children and home-making," women are still being exploited in both work and love (139).

In stressing the importance of marriage, Dell insists that it involves the work of both men and women, but that, if women are to achieve freedom and happiness, they "need an education which will enable them to relate their work outside to their love-lives in ways both realistically useful and emotionally stimulating" (353-54). Further, if a society is to prosper in the coming of age of modern ideas, attitudes, and behavior, it must cease to encourage the patterns of moral behavior that derive from Comstockery censorship; the use of drugs and quack medicines; the practice of sex as an amusement that often brings unwanted pregnancies, abortions, anxieties, and fears; and the continued exploitation of women in factories and in prostitution.

How, then, is this state of emancipation to be achieved? Not only must the young be freed "from the emotional need for parental care," but they must be educated to develop their normal "biological instincts" and to make their own choices: they must achieve a normal heterosexual relationship that has become "an increasingly selective and increasingly personal sort"; they must learn how, as ability and strength permit, to earn a living; they must achieve their own philosophy of life that is derived, not from outmoded ideas lingering in the culture, but from the earned belief that comes from experience and self-knowledge. Psychic health consists both in man's adapting to social customs and in his having respect for "the reluctance with which our adaptive efforts are made" (200). If men and women are to achieve health and happiness, they must learn to work and love and live together as responsible and informed adults. That the machine world has given man new possibilities is both a fact and a faith. Hopefully, man can overcome his struggle with famine and poverty and can learn to use science "for other purposes than those of self-destruction" (201).

While the ideas and subject matter of *Love in the Machine Age* make for a complexity in style and presentation, the book contains a wealth of brilliantly presented ideas. Throughout, Dell seems consciously aware that his use of new psychological theories and his own interpretation of facts are open to question. His application will, he writes, "doubtless require correction"; for facts about human nature have often proved to be only "dogmas about facts." Although the book was both attacked and praised, Max Eastman's comment on Dell's ideas in *Love in the Machine Age* is mostly attack. Eastman accuses Dell of living a double life, of reversing his attitude toward women, toward love, toward marriage and sex, and concludes that the book is unscientific, the work of a "charmingly irrational and reactionary neighbor of mine."[1] Whereas Dell interprets love as involving the whole emotional process of growing up, of working and acquiring a mate, Eastman interprets Dell's use of the term as literal and ultimate solution for all man's problems. Eastman is right in noting the essentially religious pattern in Dell's thinking, but the premises are based, nonetheless, on biological, historical, and psychological findings.

Love in the Machine Age is an inclusive statement of Dell's ideas and may serve best as a reference book to be consulted for guidance and information, rather than as a piece of sustained reading; but it puts in organized essay form many of the ideas on rebellion and education, on work and economics, on love and marriage, on women and idealism that had concerned Dell throughout his life and that he had dramatized in his own novels.

II   Love Without Money

By July, 1930, with *Love in the Machine Age* finished for autumn publication, Dell began a new novel; but progress was slow. As he says, "the mind works in quite different ways upon fiction and upon an essay"; the essay had demanded constant use of "scientific method"; writing a novel required creativity. He worked on his manuscript through the winter and, in early spring, collaborated with Mitchell on a new play, *Cloudy with Showers*. In May, Dell spoke at the Mental Hygiene Camp in Washington, D.C., and in June, lectured in Cleveland and Chicago. Returning to the novel, he threw away a mountain of manuscript and started over. As he says, "at last the stopped-up vein of fantasy was unplugged, and the story began to come with a rush."[2] He finished *Love Without Money* in August, 1931, and it was published in October.

The title of *Love Without Money* sounds like that of a proletarian novel of the 1930's, but it is not.[3] While part of the action occurs during the business collapse of 1920 and while the characters are personally without money, the novel is more concerned with social prejudice than with economic injustice. *Love*

Without Money is a psychological study of the recent past that Dell himself had known—a kind of fictional dramatization of many of the ideas that he had already explored in *Love in the Machine Age*. The novel portrays, therefore, the antagonisms between two generations: the "patriarchal" ideas and customs of parents and society clash openly with the plans and purposes, even the "education" of a young man and woman who are very much in love. In contrast to the normal "heterosexual" love of young Peter Carr and Gretchen Cedarbloom, Dell shows how various kinds of love—or substitutes for normal patterns—have grown from possessive and patriarchal attitudes to become part of the social matrix with which the young must cope.

Using an idea from Browning's "The Statue and the Bust" —that a "crime" serves as well as a virtue for a test—Dell plots the story of *Love Without Money* in the Midwestern town of Clark City, not far from Chicago. The action covers just over a week: from "1919, on a Saturday two days after Christmas, a few minutes past eight o'clock in the evening" until eleven o'clock on the morning of January 1, 1920. Focusing throughout the novel on the hero and heroine and their concern with work and love, Dell achieves a unity of structure and an insight into motives that make the novel one of his best about youth and rebellion. But the characters are only variants of the type Dell has already written about; Felix Fay, Rose-Ann, Janet March, and a string of others have coped with the same ideas and problems.

Love Without Money is the story of Gretchen Cedarbloom, who has grown up with money, and of Peter Carr, who has grown up without it, but who are in love with each other and in rebellion against parental authority and returning to school. Home for the holidays from Miss Quilter's finishing school, Gretchen has a "fierce pride" and a rebellious spirit that have given her notions of her own. Her refusal to return to school lies not only with its lack of freedom, but also with the cult of homosexuality of some of the students. She senses even more keenly, now that she has grown up, the domination of her mother, who spends time advising girls at the Young Women's Christian Association; she urges them to keep their virginity and to think of the "Glorious Adventure of Work" (13). The Cedarblooms live in a fine neighborhood; her father, whom she sees as a "fall-en tower," is a professor in Cope College. He has more under-standing than his wife; but both are protective of their family, and defenders of the old ways. Gretchen's real battle for free-dom and independence—going to dances and movies, having the car—intensifies after she falls in love with Peter Carr; but she has another reason: "among the many motives which had pushed Gretchen last summer into her affair with Peter was the wish to put some gulf between herself and her mother which couldn't be crossed" (156).

Peter Carr has many of the familiar characteristics of the Dell hero: he is sensitive, intelligent, interested in sex and rebellion. His family is poor; his mother, mournful and oversolicitous; his father, a Socialist of sorts—"just enough to be a failure at mon-ey-making" (33)—reads Upton Sinclair, David Graham Philips, and Joseph Medill Patterson; and he measures his son's achieve-ments by Socialist dogma, usually to find the boy wanting. Peter's older brother, as if enacting what may happen to the young in a "patriarchal" society, has become a victim: once a member of a gang and accused of stealing, the boy joined the army, only to be killed in the war. With an inclination toward books and writing, Peter has quit college to become a reporter and perhaps a poet. He has by now had a number of love affairs with married women and divorcees—just a "bit of experience to grow up on" (30). The little talk that he and his father have about women after his mother has found contraceptives in his coat pocket makes him realize how much he wants to leave Clark City. Like Gretchen Cedarbloom, with whom he is in love, he rebels against home and school.

Dell presents the genesis of Peter Carr's "rebellion" through a flashback that recounts the boy's growth and shows, in part, how his thinking has been shaped by a number of happenings and reactions. Stealing pictures from a library book, lying to receive a scholarship, and suffering remorse over his acts and over the loss of his brother have left indelible impressions; meet-ing girls and going to parties have finally led him to Gretchen and to the decision to quit school and to pursue his education in his own way. As Dell himself had done, Peter proposes to study in libraries and to learn from working with people who have had experiences and talk about them. Thus, his rebellion has brought the discoveries of love and work: the love affair has taught the boy to deal with a variety of emotions and actions which a bourgeois society usually forbids; work has made him economically and, consequently, intellectually and psychologically independent.

Although the young lovers really instruct each other, it is Gretchen who teaches Peter about love and loving. Living as they do in a world where "patriarchal" customs dictate, they must "sublimate," to use the newest term they know, their real desires. As Gretchen defines the word: "It means, when you want to do something, you do something else instead" (95). For them, it means that their place of instruction varies from a snow-covered picnic ground to a speakeasy with rooms upstairs; their sublimation includes gin drinks, Negro bands, blues singers —the standard social fare of the 1920's—and assorted conversations about love, sex, and money. Many of their discussions are case studies of family life; their own problems are those of youth of any era.

Love Without Money, then, becomes a fictional study of the manifestations and relationships of various kinds of love, some of which deserve special mention. The invitation to join the "elect" at her school and to "love" only women has forced the normally inclined Gretchen Cedarbloom to leave. At home, she observes that her mother's love, vindictive and autocratic as it is, springs, she believes, from a hatred of men; and she recalls that her brother has kept love letters from a male friend. There is the ashamed but assertive love of Gretchen's father, who actually understands the new generation in spite of his wife's dominating influence. Or there is the attitude of Peter's father, who believes in free love as long as it involves two Socialists; Mr. Hartling, the bachelor professor at Cope College, whose love for literature is greater than any adventure in life; or President Borden, whose role as "all but a Heavenly Father" enables him to radiate "wisdom, kindness, forgiveness, understanding" (148).

And Dell includes other kinds of love and lovers: the devotion of Peter's mother and sister; the love of friends; the love of success, of ideals, of position, of ability, of money. From the point of view of society, the love affair of Dick and Anne, or of Peter and Gretchen, is illicit, wrong; from some ideal point of view, the love of Peter and Gretchen is based, not on codes and customs and the legalities of society, but on the responsible choices of two individuals. As Peter says, "sooner or later . . . we have to unlearn everything they teach us as a child" (197).

Traditional customs and family ties are not, however, easily cast aside. Gretchen, remembering her mother's ways of punishment and the "magic of mothermight" with which Mrs. Cedarbloom used to conjure her children into "helpless babyhood," almost falls into the trap once more. As Dell allows Peter to see: "Life was a fairy tale with the wrong ending. . . . The Princess was imprisoned in a tower by an Ogress. And he was the Hero— only he wasn't. He couldn't slay the Ogress, because the Ogress was her mother" (167). Yet there is a way out: he can make enough money to rescue his love. He begins to write feature articles and to send them to a Chicago newspaper. Although Gretchen has a job in a wallpaper business and Peter's article has been accepted, they have, among other things, spent too many nights together above the speakeasy. As they both lose their jobs because of their conduct and manner, their thoughts of going to Chicago become both an escape and a planned venture in idealism.

Youth, Dell believes, has a hard time growing up; and Peter and Gretchen illustrate his view. Whether married or not—and they are not—and whether in Clark City or Chicago—and they choose Chicago—they must be responsible to themselves, to their love for each other. Whether a crime or not, as Browning says, such behavior becomes a test just the same. The real proof of their love and of the education that has furthered it lies not in theories but in the outcome of the test. As they rent an apartment, decorate it, and count their money, they can honestly say that they have achieved what many couples achieve—with and without money, or with and without marriage—a continuing love for each other. If the paths that brought them to this conclusion have been radical, the conclusion itself seems utterly respectable. Yet their rebellion has led them to ask and answer a vital problem: each must adapt to the world in his own way.

Love Without Money is a story about love without marriage; for, to readers in 1931, the five hundred dollars that Peter and

Gretchen possess must surely have seemed God's plenty. The problems of responsibility and sex had relevance then just as they do in the 1970's, but in the 1930's, when for many neither savings nor jobs, nor the prospect of a job, were probabilities, man's personal responsibility, including his attitude toward sex, had already become circumscribed by economics. For many, individual rebellion could neither assuage nor correct an economic world that had already crashed.

III   Diana Stair

Curiously enough as the depression deepened into the 1930's and social needs invited the attention of revolutionary and liberal thinkers, Dell turned away from contemporary experience and events for fictional subjects; he wrote his next novel, *Diana Stair* (1932), about the historical past. Yet, in returning to the past, Dell did not mean to neglect or abandon those social and political issues that had concerned him throughout his life. As he says in the prefatory statement:

In the '30s and '40s of the nineteenth century the Utopian spirit in America had its most vigorous blooming. Everything which we in the twentieth century regard as most characteristic of our times, made its appearance then; and of all periods in American history, those decades are the nearest to our own in spirit. America had more of the modern spirit then than it had for a long time after the Civil War—which cut America off from full participation in the intellectual interest of Western civilization. Before the Civil War came so near as to blot out every other interest, Americans could think and talk about the same things as we think and talk about today.

And much later he wrote to Max Eastman: "It is evocation of the past in terms of experience and emotion that has value."[4]

With an enormous cast of characters, *Diana Stair* is an encyclopedic coverage of historical events and intellectual attitudes of the 1830's and 1840's—a survey of customs and issues that includes the rise of socialism and abolitionism, the exploitation of women in mills and factories, the antagonism of capital and labor, the rise of industrialism, the intellectual ferment of the Concord and Boston circles, the Bohemianism of Paris, the social idealism that emerges from Brook Farm and other such experiments. And, as in Dell's other novels, the customs and issues, the attitudes and events become the milieu which feeds, motivates, and evokes the experience and emotion of the character. *Diana Stair* is the inner history of the heroine, Diana Stair Millburn Crocker, the portrayal of the troubled and restless search of a woman whose uncertain beliefs and shifting moral standards make her both saint and sinner to those who know her. An echo of the Greek Diana, a courageous egotist, she rationalizes her experiences, feeds on her successes, and glories in histrionics. As with the other novels, much of the book is autobiographical.

Dell had written about some aspect of what he calls his narcissistic-sexual-social conflict in all of the novels up to now, and this very conflict becomes central to the life of the heroine in *Diana Stair* as she vacillates between her impulse to live a free and unrestricted life as lover, poet, and Bohemian, and her impulse to accept the limitations and restrictions imposed by working, organizing strikes, editing, marrying. The pursuit of first one side of the conflict and then the other, along with her geographical wandering, gives structure to the novel. In the five books Diana moves from her widowed Bohemian-like freedom back into a world of routine factory work and the organization of strikes; then to a wealthy marriage and successful writing career and to a world of flattery and adulation; and finally to the pursuit of an ideal in one of the new utopian communities, where helping others and breaking established customs and laws only lead to her own arrest and trial. After 250,000 words, she accepts, at least for the time being, the "responsibilities" of marriage; she accepts life as it is.

Diana Stair, then, is the story of a woman who is "several kinds of person, living several sorts of lives by swift turns." As one life intrudes on another, her pasts are "forever bobbing up to confuse and confound her present" (75). Born into a bankrupt family—her father is a state senator in Indiana—she has been a precocious reader, has caught the spirit of the French Revolution and new social theories at Mount Holyoke, has grown up in a ferment of rebellious thought, and has trained to be a teacher. One of the small band of hopefuls, she believes that America should be not just for the smug and conventional but also for "mad idealists" and for citizens who believe in the future. More at home in this dream of a brighter America "than in its actualities," she has always felt like "an outsider in the world in which she lives" (75).

With her twofold nature, Diana has actually tried to cope with the world, but she has "other standards" with a "superior authority" and—less in defiance of others and more out of forgetfulness—she follows her own beliefs. As a Quaker, she has looked within for guidance; and, although she has made mistakes, she has retained "a conviction of her own rightness" (78). In her private world she writes letters to herself, explaining such things as "poverty or cruelty or injustice or property or money or marriage or the position of women: to a young Utopian," who is, perhaps, Diana's "childhood self" (38). But this inner resourcefulness provides both strength and refuge from the real world: her dream of a utopian world, "an imaginary and glorious Future," suggests the religious pattern of her thinking—one that also typified Dell's own thinking in his long career. But social issues are also public problems; to solve them takes any dreamer into the public arena. It had taken Dell; it takes Diana.

Actually, Diana's private dreams are public issues. As Diana Millburn, she has been a successful, militant worker in political and social organizations. Her work in the Liberty party and with the Abolitionists merits praise as if she had—like Dell in his own life—found a way of furthering publicly her own private wishes. But what at first seems a group of honest idealists to Diana becomes a fractious band that quarrels over spoils. As she sees it, Nellie Hawks wants to make the Abolitionist "platform into 'a general proclamation of Emancipation of Everybody from Everything' " (59). Disillusioned with other idealists, but not with her own ideals—as perhaps Dell had become in the 1920's—Diana can no longer "endure the vulgarities of factional intrigue and the dull practicalities of political squabbling" (77).

Several years after her husband's death, Diana returns to Boston to seek a teaching position; but her return to public life, as she finds, is marred by private habits and actions: she has the nude portrait of herself hanging in her room at the boarding-house; she smokes; she loves to shock people, to be the rebel, to do odd things; she breaks off her reasserted interest in "the Cause." As Dell himself had found, radical thinkers demand conformity just as much as anyone else. Although Diana has the

spirit and resourcefulness of her Delphic namesake, she leaves
Boston—almost as if trying to escape. As William L. Garrison has
told her: "someone must hold fast to principle. . . . You must
find your own place and do your work in humility and patience" (130). Her search takes her to the mill city of Pickering.

Actually, Diana's return to public issues is delayed by an affair with Freddy Dunn, son of a wealthy landowner and share-
holder in the corporation. Her reasoning that "life must be enjoyed while still there was time" suggests her whimsical and va-
gabondish nature. She locks up "the toys of truth, honor, justice, human decency" into the box of the past and indulges her
desire for unrestricted freedom. Then she quarrels with Freddy,
and after renouncing their affair, she turns to the problem of
mill wages and prepares for a strike. If, during the 1920's, Dell
had spoken very little on social issues, he now includes chunks
of social history as a background for Diana's actions: the labor
movement and wage problems, methods of organizing and stag-
ing a strike, slavery and abolitionism, the invasions of privacy
through seizure and search. But, when the corporation threatens
to expose Diana's character—her smoking and exotic practices—
she gives up being a savior and returns to Boston. As a mill girl
says to her: "You are in an impossible position, and you might
as well realize it. No one can have a foot in both camps, the
way you have, for very long. You'll have to make your choice.
. . ." (233) She does: she returns to her poetry; and then a series
of events lead to her marriage with rich Ellsworth Crocker.

As in *Janet March,* the man who marries the heroine is introduced about halfway through the novel: he has, of course,
his own story. Ellsworth Crocker, whose uncle owns stock in
the Pickering mills, is a would-be writer, a onetime Bohemian,
and now the publisher to whom Diana sends her poem. He has
lived in Paris among the literary, but he has curbed his youthful
ambition to write in favor of becoming a lawyer. He is sympathetic to reformers and revolutionists, but he remains a conservative. As Dell writes, ". . . his qualities were but an individual
variation upon the tendency of the generation to which he belonged" (275). He has persuaded his uncle to rescind the wage
cut at the mills, although the union has already been dropped.
Diana's illness, which accounts for her presence in the Crocker

household, is only one in a sequence of events that leads both to her marriage to Crocker and to the publication of her poem. Just as marriage gives her social position, publication of her work establishes her as a writer and introduces her to the society of both Boston and London.

To a greater extent than in the other novels, *Diana Stair* abounds in "contemporary" references: to George Sand, Chopin, William Lloyd Garrison, Carlyle, Alexandre Dumas, Orestes Brownson, Holmes, Emerson; to communism, German agrarianism, the anti-rent movement; the Mexican war; the Corn Laws; the economic depression of 1847; the abdication of Louis Philippe; the rise of socialism in France and Italy; the contention of political parties; the slavery problem; the prospects of war; and the growing unrest among the laboring classes. Sometimes historical lessons are implied: the imposed settlement by the allies in the treaty of 1814 can not endure; the peace of Metternich is only a breeding ground of new wars; for now, after thirty years, the "revolutionary pot" in France, Hungary, and Italy and even in Russia is beginning to boil. Nor can America remain isolated: ". . . the history of America is simply a part of European history" (364). The prediction that slavery will erupt in civil strife during the 1860's is, of course, an easy one; to recognize Negro or civil strife as a problem in the 1930's attests Dell's grasp of an issue that has not yet been solved.

In Book Three, Diana has been under the aegis of Emerson's guidance: "I have quite other slaves to free than those Negroes, to wit, imprisoned spirits, imprisoned thoughts . . ."; and, in Book Four, under Keats: "For I would not be dieted with praise,/ A pet-lamb in a sentimental farce!" In Book Five, Dell returns to Emerson for his quotation: "Too long shut in strait and few/ Thinly dieted on dew. . . ." Thus, escaping from the literary life of Boston "into the green peace of Concord," Diana returns for a while to simplicity, to earth, to the freedom of swimming nude, to the unlicensed rebellion that has seemed essential to her nature. She has an affair with Tristram Crocker, Ellsworth's cousin, and much thinking and remembering to do before she sees that the "world was one's home, and one had to stay in it, suffer with it, fight for it" (498). She then goes to the "Apple Farm Commonwealth" as teacher and lecturer.

As in *Moon-Calf,* Dell develops the character of Diana partly through her geographical wandering and intellectual probing, and both the wandering and the probing produce her split loyalties: she agrees with the Socialist ideal of production for use; yet she knows her capitalist husband is no ogre. She believes in the communal life but rejects dormitory living for privacy. She has practiced free love, but she now declares that she is against a "lot of silly love affairs." At the end, she accepts marriage and the "actual world"—the very conclusion and synthesis to which Dell's own "intellectual pilgrimage" had brought him.

Diana Stair, Dell's most ambitious and longest novel, is a feat of scholarship and an imaginative reconstruction of people, places, and events that relates the personal lives of the characters to the social, economic, and political issues of the times. As characters move from mill town to communal farm and from village to Boston, London, and Paris, they encounter famous historical personages, important political happenings, and social problems, and, in doing so, they make more extensive social and political criticism than is found in the other novels. But this involvement of character in public event makes the strike at the mill and the trial at the communal farm two of the best scenes in the novel. In both episodes, Dell's use of dialogue and argument gives him the chance to debate the issues of socialism and social idealism, to discuss the problems of legality and abstract justice, and to present at the same time the varying attitudes and emotional attachments of individuals: the abstract idealism of Tom Coleman of Apple Farm; the belief in struggle of the Socialist lawyer Robert Libbin; the passion for "old-fashioned" justice of Ellsworth Crocker; the near-mystical idealism in America's future of Diana.

Like all of Dell's novels, *Diana Stair* moves at a quiet, deliberate pace. Even at moments of crisis—the impending strike, the escape of the slaves, the trial of Diana and Tristram—the action is delayed by detail, qualified by description, and modified by the introduction of historical material that adds information but little depth of feeling. Dell's characters are forever analyzing themselves and each other through the omniscient voice of the author that comments and explains.

As a character, Diana Stair is almost unbelievable. What was honest searching for Felix Fay and Janet March in their limited but real worlds is for Diana Stair a series of escapades and adventures in freedom and reform that takes her from the Abolitionist platform in the beginning of the novel to the Socialist colony at the end. In between, she has been a schoolteacher, a factory girl, a free lover, a strike leader, a successful poet, the wife of a very rich Boston lawyer, a famous literary person in Boston and London, a reformer and zealous humanitarian. The few lines of the poem that supposedly shows her genius, and her little habits of smoking, of having a nude portrait in her room, of swimming in the nude seem more naughty than innovative; and, while they suggest modernity for a heroine of the 1840's, they sound more like little farcical experiences from Dell's own life, which they are. Yet the novel remains an elaborate presentation of social injustice in America's past that decades have not yet erased.

Diana Stair received qualified praise and relatively little attention from reviewers, although Dell thought it was his best novel. It had indeed cost him hours and hours of labor—sometimes eighteen a day—and constant writing and creating had put a severe strain on both his mental and physical health. When *Diana Stair* was published in mid-October, 1932, Dell was already busy with a series of lectures and was soon to begin work on his autobiography. *Homecoming* was published the last of September in 1933.

IV   Homecoming

Just as the novels had been imaginative explorations of Dell's experiences and ideas, so his autobiography is another backward glance at that same past, but with real names and places that, through the haze of memory, often seem unreal and fictional. *Homecoming* is the story of Dell's "quest for life, liberty, and happiness"; and the narrative is sensitively and honestly written. His life, he thought, was not remarkable, but as a "less conventional kind of youth"—not unlike Felix Fay, but far more arrogant and aggressive—he had finally learned to do "things that other people do." He had grown up in a "confused and difficult" world; he had been helped by such modern intellectual ideas as socialism and Freudian psychology. He had learned to make not only a living but friends, and he finally perceived that "beneath varying circumstances we are all human beings who go through much the same course of emotional adventure in growing up" (ix). In learning to accept a home, marriage, and a family, he had, in a sense, come home.

Nearly half of *Homecoming* is devoted to Dell's early life before he went to Chicago, and these chapters contain what Tanselle has called "one of the most perceptive analyses ever written of youthful feeling and intellectual development."[5] In examining his early life, Dell probes into the twists and turns of remembered experience; he tells of his father and mother, of the meaning and memory of a book read, of a friend who may have introduced him to new ideas. The chapters beginning with life in Davenport are rich with memories of writers and artists he met there, of the history-making years that included the Chicago revival and the growth and changes in Greenwich Village. Although Dell is often vague about personal relationships, especially in his love affairs, these sections contain sensitive and perceptive reminiscences of leading personalities of the period, some of them now neglected and forgotten. One of Dell's best books, *Homecoming* may well serve as source material for the intellectual life of the first two decades of the twentieth century.

Dell ends *Homecoming* with the writing of *Janet March* in 1923, although a few pages of typescript in the Newberry Library carry the story a little further. For whatever reasons, he had ended the published volume at the place where his reputation as a leader of liberal and revolutionary thinking had not yet been seriously marred by his loss of prestige in his failure to fight the suppression of *Janet March.* In a sense, the ending is right; for, in the novels that follow, he neither changed nor developed; he simply told and retold his own story with imaginative variations. The publication of *Homecoming* followed that of *Diana Stair* in less than a year. By the next autumn a new novel, his last, was ready for publication.

V   The Golden Spike

The Golden Spike, which appeared in October, 1934, is the story of the growth and education of young Harvey Claymore. The history lesson with which the novel begins and the failure of the boy to answer the questions epitomize the problems of the boy's life: a knowledge of history and an interpretation of the past may provide ways of understanding the present and the future, but is no guarantee that individuals can make accurate decisions about their own lives. One lesson of history to be found everywhere is the importance and power of money, whether in the hands of an individual or as the dream of an idealist or as part of the national development. For example, as history shows, the "golden spike" of railroad fame, which united the transcontinental rail system and tied North and West together was also the wedge of gold that split North and South during the Civil War and after.

In terms of Harvey Claymore's personal life, the "golden spike" takes on additional meaning: it is the "idea" that becomes central to his intellectual and emotional search. It contains, so to speak, the memories and problems of his early life, his idealism, his frustrations, his desire for money, and later as the problems of money merge with influences from his ancestral past—both hero and heroine are descendants of a character in *Diana Stair*—the concern for money becomes part of the "wedge" that breaks into his private life and destroys his marriage. *The Golden Spike* is a psychological study of personal idealism set against the historical background of post-Civil War America. As one character says: "too few of us realize how clearly the future of America can be read from its past" (39). The conclusion is true, but only for the few and only in an ironic way.

The story begins in the Midwestern town of Herault where young Harvey Claymore's father edits the newspaper for aging millionaire Colonel Murchison. The Claymores admire the Colonel's wealth and position and hope to be remembered in his will, but on his death, the Colonel leaves his money and the newspaper to his bigoted and narrow-minded son-in-law, Chester Ripley, who promptly hires a new editor for the newspaper. Realizing that he has always "moved in the Colonel's shadow," and that he has now become one of "the Colonel's victims," Claymore must begin life anew and on his own: the little newspaper that he buys in Minnesota is successful enough that he can send his son to college.

At college, but with little conscious awareness of his reasons, Harvey finds himself interested in the historical past of America. Writing his thesis in history and viewing history in terms of economic determinism, he conceives of the thesis idea that becomes integral to the story:

that the slave-owning South, in bringing on the Mexican War, had encompassed its own doom, through the annexation of California and the discovery of gold—which turned the attention of Northern financiers to schemes of transcontinental railroad building, and of the whole Eastern mercantile class to the developing Western market, thus shattering the compromise by which slavery had been maintained, swiftly destroying the Whig Party, creating the new anti-slavery Republican Party out of Eastern merchants and financiers and Western farmers, and thus bringing on the Civil War by which slavery was destroyed. (99)

Since the transcontinental railway had been started during the Civil War and since the last spike to be driven was supposedly made of gold, Harvey calls his thesis "The Golden Spike"—"the spike that California gold drove between the Northern mercantile-financial group and the Southern slave-owners . . ." (99-100).

Harvey's knowledge and use of the past lead to both academic success and inner satisfaction. History, which has become his "wild, unreasonable, reckless passion . . . ," enables him to "forget one's family, one's money problems, one's very honor, in the deep satisfaction of a historical thirst" (101). From this "high mountain" he has been "shown all the kingdoms of the world," and he has no desire to return to his rural newspaper job. With Professor Schulkind acting as a kind of school guide in a way that Dell had been guided by and had guided others, the boy feels inspired as if he "had just discovered something about himself" (102). In the scenes in which Harvey discusses economics and socialism with his friends, the action, as in many of Dell's novels, is mainly argument over ideas, a kind of lecturing in dialogue, which concludes that socialism may not save the world but may furnish ideas to "wake people up" (110). In using this lecture-dialogue technique, Dell has both taught a lesson in history and described the intellectual development of his hero and friends.

But an intellectual awakening is not, as Dell knows, the same

thing as having made a decision about self. With the death of his
father, Harvey must choose between remaining in college and
returning to the newspaper business. His choice is between ideals
and money; and, in choosing ideals, has he not learned from the
past that the pursuit of gold leads mainly to destruction? By
clinging to his ideals, has he not thus saved himself? Book One
ends with his leaving the town of Herault; Book Two, with his
graduation from Lockwood College. Both events constitute
an ending and a beginning.

In Book Three, Harvey's new position in the history department of Franklin College gives him a new sense of freedom.
There are teas and arguments about socialism and Nietzsche;
there are parties and love affairs. There is endless talk in the
"Carl Schnaubel" crowd, with cynical and satiric comments on
the "ridiculous sentimental taste of the last generation." But the
meeting with Marion Ripley, whom he knew in Herault and
whose family had become rich with Colonel Murchison's money,
introduces a new dimension of the past that includes money, his
father's dismissal, and family history. As Marion and Harvey discover, their mutual grandmother is Evelinda Sackett Lipscomb,
the protégée and friend of Diana Stair. Their love affair, which
ends in marriage, links them to a past that provides them with
both money and a problem. Harvey, always without money,
has married a woman of means.

Actually, Marion's money becomes an irritant that leads finally to separation and divorce. Harvey sees the handsome "hand-
me-down" furniture from the Ripley's as "preposterous gifts"
which rich people can inflict on their friends "just by making it
too obviously expensive to throw into the dustbin . . ." (360).
Marion wants to travel abroad; Harvey, to study for an advanced
degree. A trip to Herault only revives Harvey's painful memories of his lack of money; but, in a frustrated sentimental mood,
he gives the money from his father's estate to an old sweetheart,
who has lost her husband and is struggling to run the newspaper
his father once had.

Although divorce is the only solution, the fault lies not with
Marion's possession of money but with Harvey's double attitude
toward it and toward the past. Like the "golden spike," money
has become the link that holds the complex issues of his life to-

gether, yet breaks them apart. All his life he has wanted a "castle" and a "pot of money," to be like a Colonel Murchison; but he has also wanted the ideals of honesty and integrity and generosity that neither the Colonel nor, as he discovers, he himself possesses. Actually, his real problem is not money, but himself; not just the past but the future, not just the ideal but the ability to adjust to life as it really is. Although Marion still loves him, she knows that she can not live happily with him; and she later marries her old "solid" sweetheart, Ralph Drake. At last Harvey sees that he has never wanted to be a teacher, but a writer; and, with this self-honesty, he provides a fairly satisfactory answer to the "past."

Both the sales and the reviews of *The Golden Spike* were disappointing to Dell, but the criticisms remain just: the historical and economic materials, even the story of "young love come to grief," are interesting and important, but the story is too diffuse; the materials are not clearly focused. The writing remains meticulous and clear, but the myriad details need greater selectivity, and the whole narrative needs greater compression. As in *Diana Stair, The Golden Spike* has a large cast of characters; and there is a developing complexity of character relationships within the novel and even between novels, as Dell picks up characters and family connections from a previous work. This complexity of family situations and the tedium of the narration help give the novel an old-fashioned aspect.

Ideas are plentiful; familiar themes are put in new context: the importance of knowledge; the pursuit of an ideal; the problems of young lovers in finding happiness; the role of money in people's lives; the conflict between integrity and hypocrisy, between old and new interpretations of facts and experience. In his use of the "spike" image and in an occasional scene, such as that of the Schnaubel crowd with its autobiographical overtones of Bohemian life, or those about young Claymore's youth, Dell is at his best. But with *The Golden Spike,* Dell's literary career virtually ended.

VI   *In Washington*

"By 1930," Harlan Hatcher wrote, commenting on Dell's work, "the day of the 'young generation' was done, and the revolt of runaway youth to the mad ideal was over."[6]   In the changing world of economic and social crisis and of new literary tastes, Dell's influence had waned: ideas that had once excited and even shocked readers and critics no longer did so. Sales lagged. Prospects for the production of a new play collapsed; his publishers turned down his next novel. With Hitler's persecution of the Jews and with "the strange trials with fake confessions" in Russia, Dell "became painfully disillusioned about Soviet Russia."[7] Sick with insomnia and indigestion, he found it difficult to write and to earn a living. In 1935, when his old friend, Jacob Baker, an assistant in one of the new relief agencies in Washington, offered him a job, Dell accepted. At age forty-eight, with a distinguished career as editor, essayist, and novelist to recommend him, he left for Washington to become, as he amusingly said, a "minor bureaucrat."

When Dell went to Washington in September, 1935, the new relief agency for writers, actors, artists, and musicians, called the Federal Arts Project, had just been organized under Jacob Baker as a division of the Works Progress Administration (WPA). Dell's first assignment was to write a report on the work projects of a former agency. As he remembers, "those reports were possibly useful; and they were certainly improving *me.* "[8] Working at regular hours and on a salary, he began to feel better; and by January, 1936, he had been reassigned as advisory editor in the project. At last, his family rejoined him, and he settled happily into his new routine.

In addition to writing the reports, there were other duties: he wrote speeches for John L. Lewis, head of the United Mine Workers; for Harry Hopkins, director of the WPA; and especially for Mrs. Florence Kerr, assistant commissioner of the WPA and head of the women's and arts projects. He prepared broadcasts and, as head of a section of the Information Department of the WPA, taught writing to his staff. In 1938, he became chief of the special-reports section of the WPA Enforcement Division; and, in June, 1943, when the WPA was disbanded, he remained to write a summary report, *Final Report on the WPA Program, 1935-43.*

Although Dell stayed with the government until his retirement in 1947, he was not allowed to hold any government job connected with the war effort since he had once been charged with conspiring to overthrow the government. But the years had been satisfying: "I am still as proud of my governmental reports," he wrote in his diary, "as of anything I have ever written."[9]

After his retirement Dell and his wife lived in the Washington area and finally at Bethesda, Maryland, spending their summers at their New Hampshire farm cottage. By 1950 he had readied a large number of personal papers, clippings, letters, manuscripts, and photographs for deposit in the Newberry Library in Chicago, and during these years he wrote a little and maintained a voluminous correspondence with friends and writers and scholars. He worked at his poetry; although some of the poems had been published in magazines and in *Homecoming* and *Love in Greenwich Village,* he now collected them into a single typescript copy, made a tape of some of them, and deposited both in the Newberry collection. A series of illnesses led to his death on July 23, 1969. In 1963 Dell had made a codicil to his will in the form of a sonnet "to BMG," requesting that his ashes be strewn in the fields of the New Hampshire farm. His request was carried out. Had he not, as he desired, become part of "earth's loveliness forever," "young again and bold and free"?

CHAPTER *9*

In Conclusion

ALTHOUGH Floyd Dell's influence and his writings have been almost forgotten, the vision of relating man's dreams and ideals to the facts of social existence and of thus shaping a new and better world has an abiding interest that is fundamental and true. Like the characters in his novels, Dell dreamed of a world in which men could "love generously . . . work honestly . . . think clearly . . . fight bravely . . . live nobly"; and he hoped in 1926 that a new generation might begin "to formulate and erect into socially acceptable *conventions,* and where possible into laws, some healthy modern ideals of courtship, marriage, divorce, and the relation of the sexes in general."[1] Dell's own life and experience had led him to this vision; and, whether he wrote book reviews or essays, fiction or autobiography, criticism or sociology, he returned time and again to an exploration of the ideas and ideals that had impelled his own "intellectual pilgrimage." Dell was not seeking answers so much as he was forever proclaiming the vision as answer and question. In learning about himself and his art, he believed that truth and beauty and goodness come from the "commonest impulses of the human race."

Dell's own life had been characterized by the business of moving on, as if he were always making the new and necessary beginning. His wandering had enabled him to observe and be part of three vital centers of social and literary thought in America: just as he had known Chicago in the early years of the "renaissance" and Greenwich Village in its golden era, so he had known Washington at a time of great social and economic revolution. He had gone to Washington out of necessity, but he liked the WPA and looked on the New Deal as partial fulfillment not only of Socialist aims but of his own: "a better living, more freedom, more opportunity, more justice, more life."[2] The years in Washington had given stability to his life and living.

Although working for the government had ended Dell's career as an independent writer, he had neither changed his conclusions about social and political issues nor altered his personal convictions about love and marriage. Living the good life—the life of truth, beauty, and goodness—demanded personal courage and firm conviction in continuing revolutionary reform; and, while many of Dell's *Masses* friends had believed that the future of mankind rested "on the Marxian dialectical process theory of class struggle," Dell had not. Rather, he had believed then and still believed in the America of Emerson, Thoreau, and Whitman, in the socialism of Ruskin and Shaw; in the Populist reform movement; in the American Socialist party demands; and in the New Deal. He had grown up with changing America; and, as a young intellectual in an unintellectual world, he had been partly an outsider, but he had also pursued independent ideals and learned to adapt himself to the changing social world of which he was a part. In Chicago and in Greenwich Village, his ideas grew and sometimes changed; and, when he began writing his novel, he set about describing the pilgrimage that had yielded both answers and questions. As style is the man, so what he wrote and his way of writing are intimate and personal, idealistic and sensitive, factual and thoughtful, egotistical and lyrical, sympathetic and responsible. His book reviews are lively personal monologues; his essays are a tissue of individual feelings and attitudes; everything he writes bears the stamp of individual assertion in language that is straightforward and candid. As editor, book reviewer, and essayist, Dell had already made an important contribution to the literary and intellectual life of America before he emerged in 1920 as an important novelist and as a spokesman for the younger generation.

As a novelist, Dell was, reviewers observed, a careful workman, a sympathetic observer of the facts of life, a close student of psychology, a fearless realist; but he was often unselective in his material and narrow in his range. Dell regarded the novel as an "imaginative dramatization of an idea" and as the analysis of a character the writer knows very well, such as himself. And just as his first novel is autobiographical and follows closely the growth pattern of the major character, so subsequent novels repeat the same organizational pattern or a fraction of it. As a way of structuring the novel and of developing character, Dell relates the intellectual and emotional development of the characters to the geographical wandering: the stops at towns, streets, and houses are where the action and the mental and emotional growth take place.

The typical Dell character is the sensitive, lonely, idealistic dreamer (either a young man or woman), whose intellectual and emotional "pilgrimage" begins in a small town and leads, after a series of trials and experiences—mostly through talk and love affairs, and usually in a city—to an acceptance of marriage, not as a conventional institution, but as a vitally satisfying personal fulfillment. Although there is a variety of characters in every novel—newspaper men, lawyers, workers, artists, vagabonds, business men of liberal and conservative persuasion—the hero and heroine are of a special type. Felix Fay, or Dell himself, may serve as the archetypal pattern. Felix is sensitive and talented, bookish and intellectual; he is the idealist who, although interested in social problems and in fairness and equality, is mostly interested in himself and in meeting the world on his own terms. Felix is both idea and emotion, and where he wanders and how he thinks and feels give him his identity.

Although Dell had read widely about a great variety of subjects, his range of actual experience was fairly narrow and restricted; what mainly interested him in the novel was showing the emotional and intellectual growth of a character; and, when he follows his own life very closely, as he does in the story of Felix, the character is warmly alive and believable. And there are others: Mr. Windle in *An Old Man's Folly* is whimsical enough to be Dickensian and thoroughly delightful and fantastic; Michael Shenstone in *Runaway* compresses Dell's search for the ideal into a person that radiates warmth and understanding; even Diana Stair, whose range of activities makes her more caricature than character, is often lively and amusing. But many of Dell's characters—Janet March and Roger Leland in *Janet March,* Gretchen Cedarbloom in *Love Without Money,* and Harvey Claymore in *The Golden Spike*—are repetitions of Felix Fay in a slightly different setting.

Dell's particular themes and ideas are nowhere better summarized than in the titles of his novels: "moon-calf" is both nickname and attribute; "runaway" suggests both evasion and search; "mad ideal" implies integrity and pursuit; "golden spike" implies money and unity and separation. The problems of marriage in *The Briary-Bush* and of love and money in *Love Without Money* suggest three of Dell's major concerns in all of his novels. Although words like "moon-calf," "runaway," and "golden spike," the name of Felix, and the flight image in *Janet March* and *Runaway* suggest a symbolic use of language, these are mainly exceptions: Dell's writing is realistic, not symbolic. While the writing is sometimes tedious with detail, both in descriptive passages and in dialogue, it has variety and an ironic humor that leave the reader bemused rather than hilarious.

Dell's means of telling his story is the intelligent, gentle, whimsical, ironic voice in which he interprets scene and character. He stands beside his characters, displaying them with sympathy and compassion; it is this account of the impressions experienced and of the thoughts those impressions engender that arouses the reader's emotional sympathy, not only for a variety of personal and social attitudes, but also for the moral and intellectual conclusions that the hero finally reaches. Dell adopted the role of omniscient author in *Moon-Calf,* and he continued to use it in every subsequent novel. Likewise, his language, lucid and precise, is generally even and low-keyed in tone, although there are lyrical passages such as those portraying the dreams of Felix Fay and Janet March; or Michael Shenstone's discovery of the joy of earth and trees and nature; or dramatic scenes of swift action, rather unusual in a Dell novel, such as the Ku Klux Klan meeting in *Runaway,* the Red Dawn ball in *An Old Man's Folly,* or the strike and Negro escape episodes in *Diana Stair.* But there is a sameness of tone, idea, and character in all of Dell's novels; and, while the writing is always competent, it is seldom triumphant.

As readers, critics, and reviewers began to lose confidence in Dell after the suppression of *Janet March,* they began to lose sight of his vision. As he writes in the revision of *Janet March* in 1927: "it appears that these wild young women are not wrecking the social order by their behavior, so much as commencing to rebuild it upon a more secure basis of candor" (408). Dell's own purpose was very serious. If some people were shocked by

his characters' free use of sex and others nauseated by his prissy
and old-fashioned talk of "babies" and "bedroom matters," he
meant to write serious fictional psychological and sociological
studies of people and their problems in the new world of the
machine.

What Dell kept insisting was that youthful idealism and rebellion are inevitable instincts in man, that ideals can and must be
established on a basis of mutual love between the sexes, that
both men and women have a right to fulfill their normal sexual
instincts to love and to mate, and that men and women can be
ideally happy in marriage. He considered his novels to be both
art and message. He had never forgotten that he was always the
child and that children can be educated and trained with proper
methods: Dell's novels are fictional lessons in showing how personal ideals may be transformed into socially accepted habits
and beliefs; at their best, they are modern "fairy tales" which
are simply written, esthetically engaging, and morally instruc-
tive.

Dell's contribution to American letters has a threefold aspect:
as a novelist, as a literary historian, and as a personality. As editor, Socialist, and lecturer, Dell was a vital influence, especially
in the smaller intellectual and literary organizations such as the
group in Chicago, the Liberal Club in the Village, or the Provincetown Players. Although few of the book reviews and essays
he contributed to the Chicago *Friday Literary Review, The
Masses,* and *The Liberator* are available except in bound volumes in libraries, much of Dell's own story and his contributions
as a social and literary historian may be found in three excellent
and readable volumes of his nonfiction, all of them long out of
print: *Homecoming,* his autobiography and memories of many
people and places up to 1923; *Intellectual Vagabondage,* one of
the best accounts of the social and literary background of Dell's
generation that includes many personal memories and evalua-
tions of Dell's contemporaries; and *Love in Greenwich Village,*
the part fictional, part nonfictional history of the rise and fall
of the Village that Dell had known. Dell knew dozens of writers
and artists from several generations; moreover, he had helped
many—Dreiser and Sherwood Anderson, Vachel Lindsay and
Edna Millay, George Cram Cook and Joseph Freeman—in their

careers. Dell's memories and observations are, therefore, the source material of an era.

Of the novels, *Moon-Calf* remains his best known and most successful; in Felix Fay, he created a character of enduring worth in American literature. With its proclamation of rebellious assertion and young idealism that affirms, rather than denies, the novel deserves a place as a minor classic. None of the other novels is so deserving, but *The Briary-Bush* remains the best fictional study of Chicago Bohemians during the early years of the Chicago revival, although the continuation of Felix's story lacks the driving force of the first volume. *Runaway, An Old Man's Folly,* and *Diana Stair* deserve to be read, partly for Dell's vision of hope and faith in the world, and partly as a reminder to any generation that what passes for new ideas is often simply warmed-over fads and fashions from another time and place.

Floyd Dell's contribution to the American social and intellectual scene merits further treatment, and any assessment will surely focus not so much on the glamor of his youthful and rebellious ways, important and significant as they are, as on his achievements as critic, essayist, Socialist, sociologist, and novelist. If he seemed to be radical at first and then a conservative— and perhaps was—he was always the liberal thinker, always the rebellious writer, always the intellectual probing into the thought and feelings of the people that made up his real and imaginative worlds: his ideal was to live the broader, saner view that comes from accepting reality as it is and from finding simple, ordinary life filled with wonder.

Notes and References

Chapter One

1. Dell, *Homecoming, An Autobiography* (New York, 1933), p. 4.
2. *Ibid.*, p. 5.
3. *Ibid.*, pp. 6-8.
4. *Ibid.*, pp. 11-13.
5. *Ibid.*, p. 25.
6. *Ibid.*, p. 24.
7. *Ibid.*, pp. 27-28.
8. Dell, *Looking at Life* (New York, 1924), p. 146.
9. *Homecoming*, p. 57.
10. *Ibid.*
11. *Ibid.*, p. 92.
12. *Ibid.*, p. 94.
13. Harry Hansen, *Midwest Portraits* (New York, 1923), p. 212.
14. *Homecoming*, p. 119.
15. *Ibid.*
16. *Ibid.*, pp. 198-99.
17. *Homecoming*, p. 133.
18. *Ibid.*
19. *Ibid.*, p. 139.
20. *Ibid.*, p. 135.
21. *Ibid.*, p. 134.
22. Hansen, *op. cit.*, p. 209.
23. *Homecoming*, p. 148.
24. *Ibid.*, pp. 164-67.
25. Susan Glaspell, *The Road to the Temple* (New York, 1927), p. 120.
26. *Homecoming*, p. 151.
27. Glaspell, *op. cit.*, p. 181.
28. *Homecoming*, pp. 155-56.
29. Letter to Fineshriber, Autumn, 1913, en route to New

York, Dell Collection, Newberry Library.

Chapter Two

1. Letter to Fineshriber, Autumn, 1913, en route to New York, Dell Collection, Newberry Library.
2. *Homecoming,* p. 188.
3. Bernard Duffey, *The Chicago Renaissance* (East Lansing, 1954), p. 132. Also see Burton Rascoe, *Before I Forget* (New York, 1937), pp. 312-74, for comment on the literary life in Chicago as he knew it.
4. *Homecoming,* p. 190.
5. *Ibid.,* p. 191.
6. *Ibid.,* p. 196.
7. *Ibid.,* p. 200.
8. *Ibid.,* p. 201.
9. "The Literary Spotlight, XVII: Floyd Dell," *The Bookman,* LXVII (March, 1923), 66.
10. *Ibid.,* p. 68.
11. "Books," *The Liberator,* IV (December, 1921), 30.
12. *Homecoming,* p. 229.
13. Quoted by G. Thomas Tanselle, "Faun at the Barricades" (Unpublished Ph.D. dissertation, Northwestern University, 1959), p. 89.
14. Harriet Monroe, *A Poet's Life* (New York, 1938), p. 254.
15. Dale Kramer, *Chicago Renaissance, The Literary Life in the Midwest 1900-1930* (New York, 1966), p. 236.
16. Emily Hahn, *Romantic Rebels, An Informal History of Bohemianism in America* (Boston, 1967), p. 182.
17. *Homecoming,* p. 212.
18. Margery Currey's letter to Dell, Dell Collection, Newberry Library.
19. *Homecoming,* pp. 242-43.
20. Dell, "A Literary Self-Analysis," *The Modern Quarterly,* IV (June-September, 1927), 148.

Chapter Three

1. Daniel Aaron, *Writers on the Left, Episodes in American Literary Communism* (New York, 1961), p. 6. Quoted from *The Liberator,* LIV (March, 1921), 8.
2. Aaron, *op. cit.,* p. 8.

3. Allen Churchill, *The Improper Bohemians, A Re-creation of Greenwich Village in Its Heyday* (New York, 1959), p. 35.

4. Art Young, *On My Way: Being the Book of Art Young in Text and Picture* (New York, 1928), p. 130.

5. Dell, *Homecoming*, p. 272.

6. Dell, *Intellectual Vagabondage*, p. 118.

7. Dell, "Greenwich Village," *The Liberator*, I (May, 1918), 41.

8. Max Eastman, *Enjoyment of Living*, p. 444.

9. Dell, "Memories of the Old Masses," *The American Mercury*, LXVIII (April, 1949), 481-82.

10. *Ibid.*, p. 482.

11. Eastman, *Enjoyment of Living*, p. 443. Also see Louis Untermeyer, *Bygones, The Recollections of . . .* (New York, 1965), p. 33. Untermeyer recalls: "After Floyd became managing editor of *The Masses*, we grew more intimate. We argued our way through many lunches and through such topics as Art for Who's Sake, Socialism versus Bohemianism, What Went Wrong With Women's Rights, What Was Psychoanalytical and What Merely Psychosomatic. Thin and shy, Floyd looked like an attenuated Puck with the touch of a forlorn Ariel. He yearned to be a poet and had been one in Chicago, but he found it almost impossible to compose lyrics against the contradictory rhythms of New York. Nonetheless, poetry was something he felt should be put to use. 'What the Socialist Party needs,' he insisted with mock pomposity, 'is a sonneteer. As a writer I've stopped composing sonnets; as an editor I find the fourteen lines ideal to fill up small holes in the make-up. It's up to you to become the laureate of the lower classes'."

12. Art Young, *His Life and Times*, edited by John Nicholas Beffel (New York, 1939), p. 271.

13. Eastman, *Enjoyment of Living*, p. 416.

14. *The Masses*, V (April, 1914).

15. Eastman, *Enjoyment of Living*, p. 419.

16. Quoted in *Echoes of Revolt: The Masses 1911-1917*. Edited by William L. O'Neill. Introduction by Irving Howe. Afterword by Max Eastman (Chicago, 1966), p. 19.

17. Eastman, *Enjoyment of Living*, p. 420.

18. *Homecoming*, p. 251.

19. Young, *On My Way*, p. 278.

20. Dorothy Day, "Girls and Boys Come out to Play," *The Liberator*, VI (November, 1923), 30. In her novel *The Eleventh Virgin*, Dorothy Day modeled the character of Hugh Brace on

Dell.
21. Paul Jordan-Smith, "Education Made Happy," *The Liberator,* III (February, 1920), 41.
22. Dell, "The Story of the Trial," *The Liberator,* I (June, 1918), 7.
23. *Ibid.*
24. Albert Parry, *Garrets and Pretenders, A History of Bohemianism in America* (New York, 1933, 1960), p. 280.
25. Dell, "Rents Were Low in Greenwich Village," *The American Mercury,* LXV (December, 1947), 663.
26. Dell, *Love in Greenwich Village,* p. 18.
27. "Greenwich Village," *op. cit.,* p. 41. Vincent Pepe was the real estate agent for much of Greenwich Village.
28. "Rents Were Low in Greenwich Village," *op. cit.,* p. 664.
29. *Homecoming,* p. 283.
30. *Ibid.,* p. 291.
31. "Memories of the Old Masses," *op. cit.,* p. 486.
32. *Young, His Life and Times,* p. 336. Young continues: "(Actually more of us had attended the studio meetings after the indictment than ever before; postcards would arrive from the *Masses* office saying: 'Come over to B's Studio Thursday night—conspiracy.')"
33. Dell, "Conscientious Objectors," *The Masses,* IX (August, 1917), 29.
34. "The Story of the Trial," *op. cit.,* p. 16.
35. *Ibid.,* p. 11.
36. *Homecoming,* p. 317.
37. Dell, "Books," *The Liberator,* I (May, 1918), 39.
38. Eastman, *Love and Revolution, My Journey through an Epoch* (New York, 1964), p. 119.
39. John Reed, "About the Second Masses Trial," *The Liberator,* I (December, 1918), 36-38.
40. Young, *On My Way,* p. 129.
41. Dell, *Love in Greenwich Village,* p. 299.
42. Thomas Tanselle, "Faun at the Barricades," p. 203.

Chapter Four

1. Merle Curti, *The Growth of American Thought* (New York, 1943), p. 687.
2. *Homecoming,* p. 138.
3. *Ibid.,* p. 157.

4. Letter to writer, May 28, 1962.
5. *Homecoming,* p. 221.
6. *Ibid.,* p. 222.
7. *Ibid.*
8. *Ibid.,* p. 339.
9. Notes for a novel, "But We Live Now," Dell Collection, Newberry Library.
10. Orrick Johns, *Time of Our Lives, The Story of My Father and Myself* (New York, 1937), p. 245.
11. *Homecoming,* p. 339.
12. Dell's printed letter from Heywood Broun's column in Dell Collection, Newberry Library. For further discussion of the Dell-Lewis discussion, see Mark Shorer, *Sinclair Lewis: An American Life* (New York, 1961), pp. 276-78.
13. Sinclair Lewis, *The Bookman,* LIII (May, 1921), 205.
14. Ima Herron, *The Small Town in American Literature* (New York, 1937, 1959), pp. 391-94.
15. Harry Hansen, *Midwest Portraits* (New York, 1923), p. 211.
16. *Homecoming,* p. 345.
17. Letter to writer, June 20, 1962.
18. Alfred North Whitehead, *Science and the Modern World* (New York, 1925; Mentor edition, 1948), p. 207.

Chapter Five

1. "The Gossip Shop," *The Bookman,* LII (January, 1921), 574.
2. *Homecoming,* p. 361.
3. *Ibid.,* p. 346.
4. *Ibid.,* pp. 346-47.
5. *Ibid.,* p. 362.
6. Warner Berthoff, *Ferment of Realism, American Literature, 1884-1919* (New York, 1965), p. 30.
7. *Homecoming,* p. 361.
8. "The Editor Recommends–," *The Bookman,* LVII (February, 1924), 459.
9. Letter to writer, March 1, 1967. Dell had made changes: in the revised edition, he had reversed the order of Books Two and Three. In placing the story of Roger before the one of Janet, he also changed the emphasis. Some of the chapters in Janet's story are drastically revised: the chapter "Conversations and a Diary"

was re-entitled "Paul," and the poem, rich in sexual imagery and one that could have offended in the original version, appears only in part. A long portion of the diary is merely summarized. The chapter "Letters and a Meeting" was eliminated from the revised version, although part of it was incorporated into another chapter. There are other such revisions. Dell added a Postscript, pointing out that Janet is not an extreme type, and underlining what was to him an essential truth: these "feminists" are modern, but "their modernism is not bookish or theoretical, and it has come about apparently by accident, through adaptation to the circumstances of a changing world." In his life and writings, that was Dell's modernism also.

10. *Were You Ever a Child?*, p. 180.

11. From omitted sections of "Homecoming" manuscript, p. 487, Dell Collection, Newberry Library.

12. *Ibid.*

Chapter Six

1. D. Aaron, *Writers on the Left,* p. 82.

2. Max Eastman, *Love and Revolution: My Journey through an Epoch* (New York, 1964), p. 268.

3. Joseph Freeman, *An American Testament: A Narrative of Rebels and Romantics* (New York, 1936), pp. 256-57.

4. Eastman, *Love and Revolution,* pp. 223-24.

5. *Liberator,* IV (March, 1921), 6.

6. *Ibid.,* VII (October, 1924), 6-7.

7. Freeman, *op. cit.,* pp. 114-15.

8. Eastman, *Love and Revolution,* p. 194.

9. Freeman, *op. cit.,* pp. 247-48.

10. Dell, *The Briary-Bush,* p. 56.

11. Freeman, *op. cit.,* p. 266.

12. Dell, *Homecoming,* p. 337. Cf. Joseph Freeman in "The Wilsonian Era in American Literature," *The Modern Quarterly,* IV (June-September, 1927), 132: Freeman writes that "in the pages of the *Masses* [Dell] wrote what was probably the first socialist literary criticism in America." In *An American Testament* (639-40), Freeman lists the three attempts to "discuss literature and revolution in America": Upton Sinclair's *Mammonart,* 1925; Dell's *Intellectual Vagabondage,* 1926; V. F. Calverton's *The Newer Spirit,* 1925, although Freeman calls it *The New World.*

13. Dell, "A Literary Self-Analysis," *The Modern Quarterly,* IV (June-September, 1927), 150.

14. Freeman, *An American Testament,* p. 371.

15. "Contemporary American Fiction," *Bookman,* LVI (January 1923), 648.

16. Dell, "Explanations and Apologies," *Liberator,* V (June, 1922), 25-26.

17. Aaron, *op. cit.,* p. 214.

18. *Ibid.,* pp. 215-16.

19. V. F. Calverton, "Revolt Among American Intellectuals," *New Masses,* IV (April, 1929), 4.

20. Michael Gold, "Floyd Dell Resigns," *New Masses,* V (July, 1929), 10.

21. Aaron, *op. cit.,* p. 216.

22. Letter to writer, July 2, 1964.

23. Dell, "Rents Were Low in Greenwich Village," *American Mercury,* LXV (December, 1947), 666.

24. Letter to writer, July 2, 1964.

Chapter Seven

1. Dell, "Critic's Magic," *The Bookman,* LXIV (December, 1926), 448.

2. *Ibid.*

3. *Ibid.*

4. *Ibid.,* p. 449.

5. *Ibid.*

6. *Ibid.*

7. *Ibid.,* p. 450.

8. *Ibid.,* p. 449.

9. *Ibid.*

10. *Ibid.,* p. 450.

11. Dell, "Criticism and Bad Manners," *The Bookman,* LVII (May, 1923), 259.

12. *Homecoming,* p. 311.

13. Letter to writer, April 13, 1967.

14. Newspaper interview on *Little Accident,* Dell Collection, Newberry Library.

15. R. Dana Skinner, "The Play, Little Accident," *The Commonweal,* IX (February 13, 1929), 431.

16. Emily Hahn, *Romantic Rebels, An Informal History of Bohemianism in America* (Boston, 1967), p. 177.

17. "Chronicle and Comment," *The Bookman,* LXX (January, 1930), 542.

Chapter Eight

1. Max Eastman, *Art and the Life of Action with Other Essays* (New York, 1934), p. 151.
2. From omitted sections of "Homecoming" manuscript, p. 523, Dell Collection, Newberry Library.
3. *Ibid.* Dell wrote that *Love Without Money* "had two themes, social-economic and psychological; it was the story of how two young people freed themselves from the traditional influences of the old patriarchal property-marriage, and made a real marriage though an unlegalized one; at the same time it was the story of how a girl freed herself from her mother's neurotic dominance, triumphed over her own homosexual tendencies, and became an adult woman in love." See p. 523.
4. Letter to Eastman, November 1, 1953, Dell Collection, Newberry Library.
5. Thomas Tanselle, "Faun at the Barricades," p. 427.
6. Harlan Hatcher, *Creating the Modern American Novel* (New York, 1935), p. 79.
7. Letter to writer, March 13, 1964.
8. "Diaries from 1938-1947," the Dell Collection, Newberry Library.
9. *Ibid.*

Chapter Nine

1. Dell, *Intellectual Vagabondage,* p. 260.
2. Letter to Max Eastman, November 1, 1953, Dell Collection, Newberry Library.

Selected Bibliography

Those who wish to read further in Dell's writings should consult G. Thomas Tanselle's complete and extensive Bibliography in his unpublished doctoral dissertation, "Faun at the Barricades: The Life and Work of Floyd Dell" (Northwestern University, 1959), pages 487 to 605. Beginning with Dell's first published poem and listing all items available through 1958, Tanselle has identified the unsigned book reviews and essays, and has included reviews about Dell's published books and provided cross references to essays later published in separate volumes. The publication of Tanselle's bibliography would make useful and necessary material more readily available to students of Dell's work.

Special mention is made of the following sources, all listed in Tanselle's Bibliography: *The Friday Literary Review* supplement of the Chicago *Evening Post* from March, 1909, to April, 1913; and in the literary section of the *Post* until September, 1913; *The Masses* from January, 1914, to November-December issue, 1917; *The Liberator* from March, 1918, through October, 1924. There are more than 3600 items in the Floyd Dell Collection in the Newberry Library, Chicago, Illinois; this collection includes letters to and from Dell, clippings, notebooks, unpublished essays, stories, notes, photographs, tape recordings. Some items in the Dell Collection are, however, still restricted.

PRIMARY SOURCES

1. Novels:

Moon-Calf. New York: Alfred A. Knopf, 1920.
The Briary-Bush. New York: Alfred A. Knopf, 1921.
Janet March. New York: Alfred A. Knopf, 1923; Revised Edition, George H. Doran, 1927.
This Mad Ideal. New York: Alfred A. Knopf, 1925.
Runaway. New York: George H. Doran, 1925.

An Old Man's Folly. New York: George H. Doran, 1926.
An Unmarried Father. New York: George H. Doran, 1927.
Souvenir. Garden City: Doubleday, Doran & Co., 1929.
Love Without Money. New York: Farrar & Rinehart, 1931.
Diana Stair. New York: Farrar & Rinehart, 1932.
The Golden Spike. New York: Farrar & Rinehart, 1934.

2. Miscellaneous:

Women as World Builders. Chicago: Forbes and Company, 1913.
Were You Ever a Child? New York: Alfred A. Knopf, 1919;
    Second Edition with a New Preface, 1921.
Looking at Life. New York: Alfred A. Knopf, 1924.
Intellectual Vagabondage: An Apology for the Intelligentsia.
    New York: George H. Doran, 1926.
The Outline of Marriage. Pamphlets on Birth Control, No. 12.
    New York: The American Birth Control League, [1926].
Upton Sinclair: A Study in Social Protest. New York: George
    H. Doran, 1927.
*Love in the Machine Age: A Psychological Study of the Transi-
    tion from Patriarchal Society.* New York: Farrar & Rine-
    hart, 1930.
Homecoming: An Autobiography. New York: Farrar & Rine-
    hart, 1933.
Children and the Machine Age. From the Seventh Iowa Confer-
    ence on Child Development and Parent Education. Bulletin
    of the State University of Iowa. Iowa City, Iowa: The
    University, 1934.
*The Emergency Work Relief Program of the FERA: April 1,
    1934–July 1, 1935.* Submitted by the Work Division, Fed-
    eral Emergency Relief Administration. Harry L. Hopkins,
    Administrator. [Washington: Government Printing Office],
    1936.
*Government Aid During the Depression to Professional, Tech-
    nical and Other Service Workers.* [Washington: Govern-
    ment Printing Office], 1947.
Final Report on WPA Program, 1935-43. [Washington: Govern-
    ment Printing Office], 1947.

3. Plays

The Angel Intrudes, a Play in One Act as Played by the Province-
    town Players, New York: E. Arens, 1918.
Sweet and Twenty. Cincinnati: Stewart Kidd Company, 1921.
King Arthur's Socks and Other Village Plays. New York: Alfred
    A. Knopf, 1922.

Little Accident (with Thomas Mitchell). Not published. Excerpts in *The Best Plays of 1928-1929 and the Year Book of the Drama in America.* Edited by Burns Mantle. New York: Dodd, Mead and Company, 1929.

Cloudy with Showers (with Thomas Mitchell). Not published.

4. Editor

Poems [by] Wilfred Scawen Blunt. New York: Alfred A. Knopf, 1923.

Poems of Robert Herrick. Edited with an introduction by Floyd Dell. Little Blue Book, No. 701. Girard, Kansas: Haldeman-Julius Company, 1924.

Poems and Prose of William Blake. Selected by Floyd Dell. Little Blue Book No. 677. Girard, Kansas: Haldeman-Julius, 1925.

Daughter of the Revolution and Other Stories by John Reed. Edited with an introduction by Floyd Dell. New York: Vanguard Press, 1927.

Robert Burton's The Anatomy of Melancholy (with Paul Jordan-Smith). New York: George H. Doran, 1927.

SECONDARY SOURCES

Aaron, Daniel. *Writers on the Left: Episodes in American Literary Communism.* New York: Harcourt, Brace & World, 1961. Dell's relation to the radical movement of the teens and twenties is presented at length with perception and scholarly documentation.

Anderson, Sherwood. *Sherwood Anderson's Memoirs.* New York: Harcourt, Brace and Company, 1942. Anderson is not always reliable, but his comments on the Chicago years are personal, stimulating.

Churchill, Allen. *The Improper Bohemians, a Re-creation of Greenwich Village in its Heydey.* New York: E. P. Dutton & Company, 1959. Dell is given a major role in this highly readable and generally reliable account of the Village. Includes an extensive and useful bibliography of the period.

Duffey, Bernard. *The Chicago Renaissance in American Letters, a Critical History.* East Lansing: Michigan State College Press, 1953. One of the first and best accounts of Dell's part in the "liberation" movement in literary Chicago.

Eastman, Max. *Enjoyment of Living.* New York: Harpers & Brothers, 1948. Eastman's memories of *The Masses,* ending around 1916.

————. *Love and Revolution. My Journey through an Epoch .* New York: Random House, 1964. Eastman's reminiscences of the 1917-41 period includes extended references to his association with Dell as editor on *The Masses* and *The Liberator* and as neighbor at Croton-on-Hudson.

Freeman, Joseph. *An American Testament, a Narrative of Rebels and Romantics.* New York: Farrar & Rinehart, 1936. Of a younger generation, Freeman was one of Dell's early admirers, and came to know him on *The Liberator* and as visitor at Dell's house.

Glaspell, Susan. *The Road to the Temple.* New York: Frederick A. Stokes, 1927. Valuable for Dell's relationship to George Cram Cook in Davenport, Chicago, and New York.

Hahn, Emily. *Romantic Rebels, an Informal History of Bohemianism in America.* Boston: Houghton Mifflin Company, 1967. Dell receives nearly a chapter in this informally written history that describes him as a "textbook case." Sprightly and entertaining. Long bibliography.

Hansen, Harry. *Midwest Portraits.* New York: Harcourt, Brace & Company, 1923. Reminiscences of Dell in Davenport and Chicago with appreciation of the early novels.

Hatcher, Harlan. *Creating the Modern American Novel.* New York: Farrar & Rinehart, 1935. This early brief appraisal of Dell as novelist remains one of the best.

Herron, Ima Honaker. *The Small Town in American Literature.* New York: Pageant Books, 1959. First published in 1939; this critic sees Dell as one of the skeptical younger writers, whose early novels are more squarely in the tradition of small-town life.

Hoffman, Frederick J. *The Twenties, American Writing in the Postwar Decade.* New York: The Viking Press, 1955. Dell's early novels related to the mood and temper of the 1920's in brief but telling references.

Kramer, Dale. *Chicago Renaissance: The Literary Life in the Midwest 1900-1930.* New York: Appleton-Century, 1966. Dell presented as one of six major contributors to the artistic revival in Chicago: a "biography-history." Ample bibliography.

May, Henry F. *The End of American Innocence, a Study of the First Years of Our Own Time 1912-1917.* New York: Alfred A. Knopf, 1959. Dell represented as leader of rebellious young during those years of innocence, first in Chicago and then in New York. Many details are inaccurate, but Dell's contribution clearly indicated.

Monroe, Harriet. *A Poet's Life.* New York: Macmillan, 1938. Few references to Dell, but useful for understanding the Chicago scene from the 1880's through the 1920's.

O'Neill, William L. (Editor). *Echoes of Revolt: "The Masses" 1911-1917.* Introduction by Irving Howe. Afterword by Max Eastman. Chicago: Quadrangle Books, 1966. The story of *The Masses* with selections from the magazine that include several by Dell. Dell's part in the magazine seems slighted.

Rascoe, Burton. *Before I Forget.* New York: The Literary Guild of America, 1937. Knew Chicago just before and after Dell left.

Rideout, Walter Bates. *The Radical Novel in the United States, 1900-1954: Some Interrelations of Literature and Society.* Cambridge: Harvard University Press, 1956. Few references to Dell, but excellent for the period.

Schorer, Mark. *Sinclair Lewis: An American Life.* New York: McGraw-Hill Book Company, 1961. For the Dell-Lewis controversy over *Moon-Calf* and *Main-Street.*

Swanberg, W. A. *Dreiser.* New York: Charles Scribner's Sons, 1965. For Dell's relation with Dreiser in Chicago and New York.

Tanselle, G. Thomas. "Faun at the Barricades. The Life and Work of Floyd Dell." Unpublished Ph.D. Dissertation, Northwestern University, 1959. A long and thorough study of Dell's life and critical review of his writings. Some of the novels receive less extended treatment; but the early plays, the short stories, and the poetry are brought into focus. The bibliography includes all of Dell's published writings through 1958 and is a major contribution to Dell scholarship.

––––––. "Sinclair Lewis and Floyd Dell: Two Views of the Midwest," *Twentieth Century Literature,* IX (January, 1964), 175-84.

––––––. "Vachel Lindsay Writes to Floyd Dell," *Journal of the Illinois State Historical Society,* LVII (1964), 366-79.

Young, Art. *Art Young His Life and Times.* Edited by John Nicholas Beffel. New York: Sheridan House, 1939.

––––––. *On My Way: Being the Book of Art Young in Text and Picture.* New York: Horace Liveright, 1928. Delightful and amusing reminiscences of life on *The Masses,* including many references to Dell.

Index